This book is dedicated to:

Basin Book Trader
and
Karli Fussell, Owner

with
honorable mention to
Rick and Marla Edge

In appreciation for granting
the Klamath Basin Writers
use of this inviting facility
—a perfect environment—
for our group:
to hold its regular meetings,
to encourage and inspire one another
through camaraderie, shared interests,
creative writing prompts, and
thoughtful evaluations and critique
of individual writing projects.

Thank you

TABLE OF CONTENTS

Eclectic Voices from the Basin

Introduction

This is the second anthology—a collection of writings—by members of the Klamath Basin Writers. A range of topics, writing styles, genres, and themes are presented here, which include poetry, short stories, and personal essays. The range includes: real-life, mystical, humorous, suspenseful, and pieces offering resolution and redemption.

Several carry a common theme inspired by one or another of the writing prompts presented at group meetings Some of those include: writing from the point of view of an innamate object; the word "hate"; amnesia; twilight zone, and the word written on a ceramic heart, to name a few.

The group was formed in 2011, beginning with a core group of students from some of the creative writing classes at Klamath Community College, created and taught by Jo Massey Johnston. The discovery of personal growth, a wide range of creativity, and special friendships are unique. The group has grown and evolved over the years, and includes many aspiring and several published authors.

They meet every second, fourth, and fifth (in those months containing five) Monday evenings, at the Basin Book Trader. It is a perfect location, one that supports local authors, sells their books, and hosts an annual "Meet the Authors/ Book-Signing" event, and promotes the vast universe of books to the community.

KLAMATH BASIN WRITERS

The Klamath Basin Writers hold basic agreements, including respectful and objective feedback, and shared leadership among the members.

At each meeting the leader guides the meeting, including: introductions, announcements, a ten-minute writing prompt, group sharing of that freewriting, plus critique and comments on writing submitted for evaluation by individual members.

We are pleased to share this new collection with the community.

Toni Bailie

High Cascades Christmas

Frigid winds whipped snow around the eaves of a snug log cabin, nestled in the trees on a small island in the middle of Vogel Lake. High in the Oregon Cascades, a trapper's family found a haven in the wilderness. In 1951, I was the five-year-old daughter of that family wintering in the Mink Lake Basin.

Our adventure began with a marauding bear. It ended with a narrow escape from death when a howling blizzard pounced on us as we hiked out of the mountains.

Dad trapped the elusive marten whose lair is deep snow country. He hiked miles of trap line on snowshoes, braving all kinds of weather. The cabin at Vogel Lake, with a rock fireplace and wood cookstove, became one of his favorite base camps. We accessed the island with a raft in warm weather and walked across the ice in winter.

Hired packhorses hauled supplies to the two-room cabin. A bear ransacked the first load of food. The curious bruin swam to the island, broke a window, and trashed the cabin, devouring all the food. He even punched holes in evaporated milk cans and slurped the contents. A few weeks later, after we arrived, Dad trapped the marauder and our family feasted on bear steak, roast, and sausage.

After this first skirmish, danger seemed far away as we settled in. Imagine the savory aroma of a bear roast wafting from the wood stove, warm bread and apple cobbler waiting on a pantry shelf.

With a whoosh, a gust of wind blows a weary trapper through the door. He shrugs out of his heavy pack and props his snowshoes against the cabin wall. "Something sure smells good," he says. "I'm so hungry my belly button's hitting my back bone."

"Daddy's home!" I elbow my two-year old sister out of the way so I can be first to clamber onto Dad's lap. Soon we gather around the table and dive into the delicious dinner. Let

the wind blow and the snow fall. The bold advance of heat from the fireplace sends cold air scurrying into the corners of the room.

The mellow glow of the kerosene lamp recalls pioneer days. But in 1951, few women with two preschoolers would follow a trapper husband into the wilderness, thirty miles from the nearest plowed road. Mom, Wyoming farm girl, did just that in spite of dire admonitions from family and friends. Mom's day formed a pattern of washing diapers in a big tub, baking and cooking on a wood stove, and riding herd on me and my sister.

We arrived at Vogel Lake in late October and planned to hike out in time for Christmas at my grandparents' home in Crescent.

Our return journey began on a clear blue day. We zipped along, with Dad pulling my sister on a toboggan. She was firmly wedged into a packing crate and slept most of the time. We spent the first night at Muskrat Lake cabin, after a six-mile trek. I entertained myself breaking icicles from the cabins' eaves.

Going was rough next morning. Downed timber hindered the toboggan. By 4 p.m. a blizzard was howling around the shores of Cultus Lake. Dad was exhausted from breaking trail in the heavy snow and towing the toboggan. As darkness quenched hopes of reaching Cow Camp, Dad started a campfire. Then we huddled miserably in our two-man nylon tent.

At dawn, we swallowed some hot soup and bread, and headed into the teeth of the blizzard. I remember trudging down the road in my mother's snowshoe tracks while 60-foot lodge pole pines writhed in the wind, and treetops came cracking down to earth. At Cultus River, Dad waded across with me in his arms. Then he and Mom inched the toboggan across a narrow footbridge.

Mom began breaking trail, sinking in about a foot each step. She developed a slow rhythm: take a step – shake the snow off – take a step. Dad struggled with the toboggan, which was sinking deeply into the snow. Mom feared that Cow Camp cabin might have burned down, but Dad kept assuring her it would be there.

At the Deschutes River, Mom waited what seemed a thousand years while Dad forged ahead and found the cabin intact. When we straggled into shelter, Mom went to pieces, crying and pacing the floor from fatigue and relief.

Dad shot a snowshoe rabbit and Mom fried the rabbit for dinner. We found a few rations in the cabin to supplement the meal. Dad surveyed the table and said, "This is what it means when we say, 'Give us our daily bread.'"

The following day, Dad stocked the cabin with firewood. He started hiking to Fall River fishery to get help. Meanwhile, Mom fought back fears of what would happen if Dad met with an accident and didn't return. For two days, she rationed food and tried to keep me entertained with stacks of magazine she found in the cabin. We both drooled over the pictures of delicious food that seemed to dominate every page.

Finally, two days later we heard Dad hollering as he approached. We dashed out, joyful, and hugged him and his friend, Walt who had come to help. On Christmas Eve, after a day's easy snowshoeing in clear weather, we reached Fall River Guard Station. But on the way out, Walt's pickup foundered in deep snow a mile from the cabin.

At age five, my biggest worry was how Santa Claus would find me. That was the furthest thing from Mom's mind as she struggled to work the switchboard of an ancient telephone. She finally made contact with my grandparents in Crescent.

On Christmas Day, another friend chugged up the road in his four-wheel drive to rescue us. When we finally arrived at my grandparents' house, I discovered—to my relief—that Santa Claus hadn't overlooked me after all.

Eclectic Voices from the Basin

Autumn Equinox

The lake wears diamonds,
Aspen wear shimmering gold,
The sky flaunts a cape of cobalt blue.

Wind swoops down from the ridge,
a cold breath foretelling coming storms.
For today, the sun spins out
the last threads of summer,
weaving a tapestry embossed with soaring osprey,
avid fishermen, a scampering chipmunk.
Toss the coins of your yearning
into the well of autumn's splendor.

MEMORIES OF A LOGGING CAMP

On my 7th birthday in 1953, Mom led me out to the garage. I discovered a bicycle with shiny blue paint and streamers attached to the handle grips. They fluttered in the breeze as I pedaled along. But first I had to master the art of balancing on two wheels. On my first forays, I tumbled off after wobbling a few feet. I scrambled up and kept trying. Finally I pedaled smoothly, exhilarated as I glided along.

We loaded my new bike into the back of our red and white station wagon. Mom steered the car north on Highway 97, skirting Klamath Lake. I noticed white pelicans bobbing near the shore. We climbed the hill above Spring Creek, into the jack pine forest that grew out of pumice spewed from the ancient eruption of Mt. Mazama. At the junction, we drove west on a ribbon of highway unspooling up toward Diamond Lake, cupped beneath the skirt of snow-capped Mt. Bailey.

We entered the verdant Umpqua Forest of towering Douglas Firs. The sun-dappled forest floor was woven with fern fronds. After a few miles, we turned into the gravel road leading to Briggs' logging camp where Dad cooked for a crew of hungry timber fallers, choker setters, and cat operators.

We negotiated the circular drive, passing two spacious houses where the higher echelon of the logging company lived. One-room cabins for the working men were strung like green beads on a necklace. Dad's cabin sat next to the large cook house. There he was the maestro of the kitchen. Lumber camps served hearty meals. The men wouldn't stay in a camp that scrimped on the grub.

Dad presided over the big grill and oven, serving up breakfast of ham, bacon, eggs, and hot cakes. As a special treat, he fried up maple bars. After breakfast, the loggers clustered around a side table to pack their lunches: thick sandwiches and slabs of apple or cherry pie. At dinner

16

the crew bellied up to tables loaded with steaks, roasts, and potatoes.

I came to spend a couple of weeks with Dad. I was adopted by Jean, the camp caretaker's wife. Her husband, Dutch kept buildings repaired and the grounds weeded. Jean was in her 50s. Her brown hair, worn in a short bob, was streaked with gray. Jean loved kids, although she never had any of her own. She welcomed me into her kitchen. I stood on a stool that boosted me level with the counter. We baked batches of chocolate chip cookies. I liked to play with her orange tabby cat who sprawled in the sunshine. He could be enticed into a game of stalk and pounce with a piece of paper tied to a string.

Jean's nieces came for a visit from the Midwest. Jane and Mary were plump blond sisters with warm smiles. Jean and Dutch planned a trip to the Oregon Coast and the Redwoods. My parents allowed me to go along. We camped overnight in the Redwoods, marveling at the towering giants. Then a fog bank rolled in from the ocean and chilled our outdoor picnic.

On the return trip, we stopped in Medford. Jean took me to J.C. Penney's and let me pick out any outfit. I was excited because I didn't get brand new clothes very often. I chose a turquoise circle skirt with matching short-sleeved blouse. I felt like a peacock in my new finery.

Briggs'camp was populated with colorful characters —tough loggers who fell giant trees, limbing them, then carting them to the landing. The logs were piled on the trailers of waiting trucks. Old Charlie was the camp bull cook. He changed the bedding, swept out the cabins and kept the outhouse clean. Dad took old Charlie under his wing. Charlie liked Dad, but snarled at everyone else.

Dad arose at dawn to prepare breakfast, then slept in the early afternoon. One day, after his nap, Dad walked down the path to the outhouse and discovered a young Stellars Jay fallen from its nest. Dad took his red bandana, scooped up the bird, and brought it into the cabin. He fed it bits of food. Soon the young bird grew bold and sassy, fledging cobalt blue feathers and a cocky top-knot. He perched on a shelf where he could see his reflection in a small mirror. He preened like a dandy grooming himself for a hot date. Dad called him Knucklehead and we often chuckled at his antics.

Alas, poor Knucklehead met a tragic end. When I accidentally left the cabin door open, Knucklehead escaped, intoxicated by the freedom of the open air. We chased after him but he eluded us. In confusion, he flew into the outhouse and fell down the stinky hole. Dad fished him out and gave him a bath. Sadly Knucklehead didn't recover from his traumatic escape. When he sickened and died I feel remorse for my carelessness.

During the 1950s there was an influx of laborers from Arkansas and Oklahoma. Dad's cryptic comment was: "If Oklahoma is the land of opportunity, why are so many of them coming to Oregon?' Two of these "Arkies," Maggie and Beacher Carr, assisted Dad in the cookhouse. Maggie was a buxom blond, with upswept curly hair and a jovial laugh. She pitched in to help, plunging her hands into the dishwater in the big sinks, scouring plates, silverware and big cooking pots. Beacher scrubbed the floors and cleaned the dining room.

One day I want to help in the kitchen, so I grabbed a mop and started swabbing the floor. I brought my arm under the end of Dad's work table where he stored his carving knives. I slit open my forearm and blood gushed everywhere. Dad grabbed a clean dish towel and pressed it on the wound. Mom fired up the station wagon and drove me sixty miles to Klamath Falls. Dr. Erlandson stitched up my arm and I still bear the scar.

In this mechanical age, logging camps have faded into the mists of memory. I vividly recall my summer at Briggs' camp, picking huckleberries with Jean as we meandered along the creek, and peddling my new bike around the circular drive. The buildings disappeared many years ago. When I drive by on the Umpqua Highway, I try to find the old camp entrance, but the forest has reclaimed it.

INTERMEZZO

February turns her back on winter,
conducting a dress rehearsal for spring.
Folded hills crouch on tawny haunches,
Cattle curl up in the mellow sun—
black commas punctuating
a tan field's declarative sentence.
Swaying cottonwoods
applaud the lengthening days,
their burgeoning buds eager to unfurl.
Chattering blackbirds gossip in the branches,
while giggling kids
bounce on a trampoline like Mexican jumping beans.

My heart jumps up
and shouts, "Bravo!" "Encore!"

ONE WEEK IN MAY: OREGON HIGH DESERT

All winter the gnarled cottonwoods leaned on the shoulder of dawn like old dowagers. Now, resplendent in gauzy green leaves, they're twirling into the dance of spring. Swollen by snow melt, the Chewaucan River no longer meanders sedately through the valley. It has become a boisterous charger, surging with renewed energy.

Five tawny fox kits emerge from their burrow, pointy ears and noses on alert. Mamma fox streaks across the meadow, her white-tipped tail floating behind like a slip-stream

Over the back fence, a dashing sorrel colt with a white star on his forehead nibbles apple slices from my outstretched palm and I stroke his silky-sleek neck. Spring flirts with me, now a sun-warmed smile, now ducking behind a lowering cloud. But the pink froth of apple blossoms insist that it really is spring.

We bid adieu as we celebrate the life of Jean, a Paisley resident since 1960. After the memorial service, I admire Cheyanne Rose, Marsha's new granddaughter. Marsha's face radiates joy like a warm lamp illuminating the window of a house recently buffeted by storms.

Dandelions riot in the lush grass of our neighbor's yard. My heart skips, recalling childhood fun. We would fashion necklaces from the cheerful yellow blossoms or make a wish and blow fluffy seed pods into the wind. The dandelion is also a flower.

Sunlight behind tattered clouds casts undulating shadows across the hills. A memory bobs to the surface. I was ten years old when Dad trapped beaver at a ranch on the Sycan River, staying in the old farm house. Mom, Susan and I came for the weekend. After dark, dad set the bright propane lantern on a table and staged a show for us. The light cast the shadows of his hands onto the wall, as he conjured up a rabbit, a bear, and an old man with a jutting jaw.

On Sunday morning I hike up the high road under mutable clouds. Wild flowers splash the hillside with vivid purple, yellow, and orange. Blue-green sage becomes a burning bush, ignited by the scarlet flame of Indian paint brush. A pair of hawks wheel overhead, coasting on invisible thermals.

I perch on a rocky crag. Below me, the river threads its lacy ribbon through the canyon. Beyond the river, a massive hillside looms against the sky. Its rocky spine reminds me of a slumbering dinosaur. I imagine it rousing from eons of sleep on huge haunches. Uprooted junipers cascade off its flanks as it lumbers out into the Chewaucan Valley.

Far from being a barren place, the high desert is filled with enchantment at every season of the year.

MY CHURCH

I worship in the cathedral of Ponderosa pines.
Sandhill cranes warble a morning hymn.
Coyotes deliver a sermon
about receiving the bounty of the land.
Butterflies bow in gratitude to wild flowers,
while soaring hawks bear my soul aloft.

KLAMATH BASIN WRITERS

Erin Barker

I WISH I DIDN'T HATE YOU

I wish I didn't hate you
And everything you do
I wish I could escape
All these feelings I'm going through

I wish my heart was softer
I wish I didn't feel
So angry, so disappointed
I wish that I could heal

Oh, God, help me heal

I think back to a time
When we both were young
We were happy and carefree
And life still was fun

But as time went on
Something happened to me
You put me in a cage
And you wouldn't let me free

No you wouldn't let me free

You silenced my voice
And I forgot to sing
You laughed at my dreams
And you clipped my wings

Yeah, you clipped my wings

But over time
My wings grew back
To their full length

And once again
I began to feel
Their strength
Then I opened up my mouth
And out came a song
And my heart began
To sing along

I wish I didn't love you
Cause now my heart is grieved
Because I equally hate the thought
That one of us has to leave

Why won't you just leave?

I wish I didn't hate you
But now as I fly
I hope I can forgive you
But for now, goodbye

Cause over time
My wings grew back
To their full length
And once again
I began to feel
Their strength
Then I opened up my mouth
And sang a new song
And my heart began
To sing along

I wish I didn't hate you
And everything you do
I wish I could escape
All these feeling I'm going through

All these feelings

HAPPY ENDING

I see the path that's set before me
I close my eyes
And imagine what could really be
If I could just believe
If I could just be free
To believe in me

The dreams I had
Plans I made
Opportunities I let fade
And slip off the horizon
Just a girl, I was afraid
Of the failures in my way

But not today

I am the writer of my destiny
With every thought I think
And every word I speak
I am creating
Though impossible
As it may seem
I will pursue my dreams
Cause this is my story
And I will write
A happy ending

I have the paper
Out in front of me
The pen is in my hand
So I begin to write the story

Of who I want to be
The past behind me
A new beginning

So I write a song of love
Everything I've ever dreamed of
Blessings from above
A brand new me
I am happy
I can finally see
I just had to believe

I am the writer of my destiny
With every thought I think
And every word I speak
I am creating
Though impossible
As it may seem
I will pursue my dreams
Cause this is my story
And I will write
A happy ending

THE OTHER SIDE OF ME

Please forgive me
I don't know
How I could go
From feeling so alive
To just wanting to hide
Dying inside

Please forgive me
This is not me
What you see
Does not reflect
The impossibility

How can you know
What I won't show
There is a part of me
You'll never see
Forgive me

Let today
Be the new day
I've been praying for
Let me be
A brand new me
What am I waiting for
All I adore
Is on the other side of me

Please forgive me
I have become my worst enemy
The wars I've won
The race I run

Things I've done
My special son
Are wearing down on me
I am not free

Let today
Be the new day
I've been praying for
Let me be
A brand new me
What am I waiting for
All I adore

All I've dreamed of and more
Is on the other side of me

Just on the other side
The other side of me

It Doesn't Have to End Here

There were times in my life
I just wanted to die
Chasing that high
Just getting by

I felt as though
I just couldn't go
On one more day
Living that way

No solution in sight
Losing the fight
Living a lie
Why even try

The easier cup
Is just giving up
I have to remind
Myself all the time

It doesn't have to end here
It doesn't have to end here
Don't throw it all away
There's a better way
Don't abandon your dreams
It's not what it seems
You've gotten this far
And fought so hard
Doesn't have to end here

Then there are times
I'm glad I'm alive
Glad I survived
Rejected the lie

Things I've not done
Songs I haven't sung
A race that's half run
Cannot be undone

We all get to choose
To give up and lose
Or pick ourselves up again

It doesn't have to end here
It doesn't have to end here
Don't throw it all away
There's a better way
Don't abandon your dreams
It's not what it seems
You've gotten this far
And fought so hard
Doesn't have to end here

Cause once it is done
Your pain isn't gone
You just pass it on
To everyone

They'll all ask why
And have a good cry
Say their goodbyes
Go on with their lives

Then you'll just be
A sad memory
That's all you'll ever be

It doesn't have to end here

ONE DAY AT A TIME

I wake up to a brand new day
Hoping things will go my way
I have a feeling that I may
Find the change I seek today

Worn out I still run the race
Careful not to slow my pace
Or fall on obstacles I face
I come in last but win first place

Thank God I didn't lose my faith

So I go on
I take it day by day
I sing a song
It gets me through today
It lifts me up and helps me
Cast the doubt away
So I go on
I go on
Taking one day at a time

Something about getting old
Trading silver for my gold
But the greatest gifts I'm told
Are those that can't be bought or sold

Now I watch the seasons change
Nothing ever stays the same
But Mother Nature has a way
Of taking us back home again

We're on our way back home again

The Winds of Change
Whisper in my ear
They sing a song
Though the words aren't always clear
Still the sweet melody
Erases all my fear
And I go on
I go on

Taking one day at a time

KLAMATH BASIN WRITERS

Brian Keith Ellis

Hang in There

I step through time
Look back on a life
The follies of a child
Or did he know more than me?

The chill is still in the air
Tendrils of mist on the pond
Trees not yet recalled to life
Spring arrives late in Maine

Stone squeaks beneath my shoe
Dips away toward the water
Stark arms of oak curve above
A hundred gnarled fingers reaching

Reaching into the past
At least that was what I thought
But as I step into my own long-faded footprints
I know I'm here to give, not receive

And so, eyes closed, arms outstretched
I summon what psychic dust I have
I hold a single thought, so clear and so pure
And sail it with love across the ocean of time

"Hang in there"

In the shadow of a president stepping down
My much smaller feet patter the ground
Chores are done, the sun is high
The stately oak shades this boy

Happiness sings in his life, my life
At least here at base
Where no one can tag you out

And somehow everything makes sense
Stones skip across sparkling water
Laughter echoes among the pines
A canoe whispers by with the neighbor boys
My heart pounds with a tug on the line
From the future, I feel a tug on my heart
Challenges to come boy, challenges to come
So I'm giving you a gift, little one
To hold tight to in the loneliness of the night

"Hang in there"

So that weekend when you're 17
And everything is life or death
And the first girl you love so madly
Cozies up with your best friend

"Hang in there"

Because one day you'll find
That you're real hope and dream
Contrary to what you feel in that moment
Is that we all go home happy

And when you find your soulmate
The first time, you know the one
With the honey hair and the playful mind
But you're too shy to hear "yes" or "no"

"Hang in there"

There's no way you'll believe it then
But if you walk that winding road
You'll find that you get second chances
And even "no" can be sweet music to your ears

And when your best friend skips out on you
To whatever heaven awaits
Without saying goodbye
And regret hangs like an unending smoky pall

"Hang in there"

How could you know in that haze
That a good wind will clear the way
And friendships so deep and so loving
Will fill the air like the scent of roses

And when your marriage and your life
Crumble around you
Like a sand castle in the rising tide
And you're bereft of love and peace and even hope
"Hang in there"

One day, near the very spot you stand
You will hold in your arms a woman
Of such incredible beauty and laughter and wisdom
And she will like it

And so, little man, in these and other moments
When it seems like the message I'm sending you
Is as far off as a distant peak, remember
Someday it's the challenges that will seem far away

And you'll rejoice in the lives of your own children
And sail through the seas of an effortless life
And the love and laughter of friends will surround you
And the touch of a lover will make your soul sing

And as I finish sending my message of love and of hope
I hear an aging, yet familiar voice of deep love and wisdom
Drift toward me like an autumn leaf on a gentle wind
To settle lightly into the curve of my ear

"Hang in there."

Eclectic Voices from the Basin

THAT'D BE ALRIGHT

Running down a lonely road
Manhattan Kansas at two in the morning
Overcome with a fear so deep and so complete
Is this my last moment on Earth?
If it is, it's definitely not alright

How could a heart so full of love
Beat in such peculiar fashion
Is this beat the last, or this one, maybe this one?
How could I have reached this moment
With nothing to show for my life?

Seconds passed to minutes, minutes to hours
Hours to days, days to weeks
Still here!
But still the race is on
The race against the reaper

I need something to hold up to the world
I need something to hold up to myself
Something to hold up to God
Something to show I had meaning
Before I walk the reaper's road

But what would that something be?
What would be enough to show a life had meaning?
Do I have to write a screenplay?
Do I have to make a movie?
Do I have to be Spielberg?

In the end, of course, nothing was enough
Houses with views
Cars without rooves
Trips on a cruise
And furniture too
So much fucking frustration
So much damn hesitation
A full house and an empty soul
Longing for that elusive meaning
Searching at the bottom of a bottle

Scraping at the bottom of a life
Shit, time to start over, hello square one
Goodbye house with a view
Goodbye car with no roof
And trips on a cruise, and furniture too

Hello tears
Hello regret
Hello fears
No sanctuary yet
Hello first step

When I looked down the path, it seemed so long
And with each step it seemed to look longer
But a funny thing happened
A very strange thing indeed
The longer the path seemed, the more I enjoyed it

Who was this person who appeared in the mirror?
The eyes looked different, even through the tears
There was an uneasiness that was lacking

Where had I lost that?
Hmmm, maybe I won't miss it
I realized I was carrying a tremendous load
Expectations from youth, unfulfilled
A longing for love, unrequited

A need to affect, unsubstantiated
But regrets and fears, yeah, those were fully realized

Set it down, brother, just set it down
Time to spin the mirror
And own what's mine
The unfulfilled, the unrequited,
The unsubstantiated, the regrets and the fears

Own 'em and then let 'em go
Time to step into Oz, no, even better than Oz
Time to walk the fields of Heaven
Where fear feels like some silly memory
And regret, a fading echo

All the things once out of reach
Swim and swirl around me
They wanted to be here all along
Just sat waiting for the slow learner
Now they're as happy as I am

Friendships and loves become easy and fun
Psychological landmines are easily sidestepped or diffused
Lifestorms that once brought stress and the urge to flee
Are handled effortlessly
The mirror spun, now I have become the hurricane

41

All around me are best friends
There is laughter that I can hear
The tears all come from happiness
They are a liquid celebration of new life
There is nothing that isn't absolutely beautiful

And in the warm reflection in your eyes, best friend
I see a promise of life yet to come
New heights to be explored
New loves to be discovered
But never needed

I marvel at the possibilities around me
An imagination-driven machine in the forge of souls
And in wrapping my arms around you
I feel a serenity within me that is indestructible
You are what angels dream of becoming
I lean on the railing, my senses are wide open
A scent of forest, a memory of touch
I feel a love so deep and so complete
If this is my last moment on Earth
Well then...yes...that'd be alright.

THE OCEAN'S EDGE

Before me stands a great ocean
An ocean I know well
I have spent my life upon its eternal back
I have been caressed by its peaceful waters
Been tossed skyward by its fury
Though I was not its target

I'd hoped it had passed into my wake forever
But here I stand
Facing it again
On this endless beach
Where once I landed
With so much hope and excitement
The ocean, indifferent
Rolls slowly against this sandy shore
The soothing sounds of its whitewash
Belie the nature of its existence

I awoke from childhood
To find myself treading water
In a Great Storm
My survival was a matter of question
My world was wind and waves and choking salt
But in time, the Storm began to pass
And I began to glean
From my constant companion's waters
The battered flotsam that would become my raft,
Save my life
Let me learn the ways of my new home
And for decades I slipped across its surface
Learning, learning, and understanding

43

Through the years my raft changed
From understanding I built a fine sailing ship
I cut the waves with grace and speed
I learned to avoid the storms
To find the smooth waters
To study the life beneath
The clear, blue surface
To feel the gentle roll of its skin
And I understood this was not my home

But as the years rolled like the ocean itself
I came to realize
That I might never find the shore
I continued to search, alone
Sometimes the ocean played tricks
Sometimes I thought I could see land
And my sailing ship would fly through the waves
But my heart would sink
It was clouds, driftwood, a far off flock
And the years passed, one by one
Learning to know myself and this ocean
The only things that kept me going

And then one day
It wasn't clouds, driftwood, or a far off flock
Just
Like
My
Dreams
It appeared in front of me
And tears of joy fell from my eyes
Like a soothing shower on a scorching day
When I felt its magnificent, sandy shore
And saw its forest-laden hills
For I had come home at last
And could leave my friend ocean behind
Forever

Among the trees and rivers we walked
Unburdened by the weight of the world
No match for our strength
Hand in hand
You, the only stable ground in my life
Your skin, soft and soothing as the sea breeze
My head turned circles
Like the wheeling seagulls above
When our lips met, fluttered
With my heart, recalled to life
Such ecstasy!
My life, my Love, exploded
A pounding surf on the shore
I can feel it even now
In my heart
In my head
In the pulse in the tips of my fingers
I was alive!
And we, in our Happiness
Slipped away from the rest of the world
Sheltered in our harbor
I felt contentment so complete
Staring into your gold-veined eyes
Until we both cried from sheer Joy
And amazement
How could two souls be so Happy
As the warm wind blew through our window
I ran my grateful hand through your hair
As you slept
I watched the peace in your face
And I felt it in my soul
We were protected in our harbor
Untouchable
Invincible
Immortal

For time truly stood still
And our Peace
And our Happiness
Were such that the Gods were jealous
And in those nights as I watched you sleep
Angel-like
I Loved every nuance
Of your innocent-girl face
Every pool and eddy in your cascading hair
Every sweet line of your sleeping form
And as you slept
Your soul told me stories
Of picnics in the sun
Little league games and piano recitals
Laughter in the dark
And you in my arms
Growing old together
Hand in hand
Our dreams and realities
Melting together
Like the azure blue of the deepening sea and sky
On an impossibly clear day
Destiny had whispered in my ear
But the words were whisked away
By a rising northern wind

And suddenly, through no fault of yours
Or of mine
I found myself on this shore again
And the great, swelling sadness of this moment
Has ripped the shattering sobs from my body
As I stand at the ocean's edge
The end of my world
From the sand, a wraith-like mist
Flows out to sea

Within it I can see visions of the future
Of watching a daughter grow up
Of porch swings and lazy, carefree afternoons
Fading...
Fading...
Like my memory as I grow old
Ghosts of a future that never was
And my tears reach the sand again on this beach
This time in a sadness
That only a Moses could know
To search one's life for the Promised Land
To touch it with your eyes
Yet never reach it
The soles of my feet feel every grain of sand
They long to grasp it, hold it, never leave it
But the time has come to go
I look back one last time
The sight of you emblazoned on my soul
You will always be who I am
The hills, the forests, the rivers
I leave all that I am now
And turn back to the ocean

So here I stand
On this endless beach
Where once I landed with so much hope
And excitement
And as I push off into my ocean
My fingers reach down to grasp
A handful of sand
This and my memories
All I have left of you
My Love.

Klamath Basin Writers

Mark H Gaffney

SIX SONNETS

Eclectic Voices from the Basin

1
The simple pleasure of your company
was everything in which my heart delights.
Your lilting voice like some epiphany,
the promise of a hundred carefree nights.
Each playful syllable a fond caress,
each word a song, and in your childlike charms
a world of feeling I could not express
until I wrapped you in my aching arms.
How sprightly you appeared upon the deck,
your impish smile, your knowing look a dare.
I coaxed you gently once upon the neck,
your slender fingers in my wavy hair.
My hand upon your flushed and heaving breast.
Another urgent look, and we undressed.

2
A noble thought for this or any age.
How to unfold the measure of a man,
engendering the wisdom of a sage
in but a blink of time, a human span.
Advice to ardent seekers of this grail:
beware the phony counsel of "the wise"
who caution you to death, an epic fail.
A stoic takes whatever will arise
for grist. The passion play of life-as-dance
demands a plucky gambit every day.
The anti-hero who fills out his pants
applies the principle of come-what-may.
Libation of the truly wise: a song
as wild and free as a man's life is long.

3
When love goes bad there's nothing to be done.
As day winds down and shadows climb the wall
we empty out and darkness bars the sun.
For want of pride how far a man can fall.
Discordant strokes of enigmatic time
belie the passing of too many years
for wanton fate to smile upon my prime.
Plain spoken words offensive to her ears
I'd sooner shout into a vagrant wind
than wallow in an unrequited love.
So, what's a pretty face if not a friend?
All things abide among the stars above.
The silent dusk presumes resplendent power
and by her leave allays the private hour.

]4
What playful sound is this upon the air
that lifts our hearts and tempts us to rejoice
in sound itself? A fiddle and a hot guitar,
a quirky girl whose soft melodic voice,
now fading to a whisper at the end,
downloads the music of the spheres——where from?
Now, calling for the angels to descend.
I think an angel has already come.
Don't bore me with your existential dread.
I'll take this smiling girl with the hardware
dad and the lunch pail lullabies to bed.
Mysterious and rare, an upbeat prayer
the likes of which——who can say if heaven knows?
Don't miss her trailer rainsong, October Rose!

5
You learn to love the qualities of stone.
Its constancy and mass, and never dull.
A roadside attraction. My pickup full.
The satisfaction of a job well done.
We place the plywood forms in parallel,
a future wall defined in empty space.
The doorway arch a doubly vacant place.
The pile of rocks goes in the hole. Next, shovel
in the viscous Redi-mix, done in haste.
Concrete and stone in equal parts, plus sweat.
Six hours of work, and then, a week to set.
I'll write my epitaph with stone, in trust
that one fine thing, if not these words, will yet
remain when flesh and blood have gone to dust.

6
Had I a steady mind upon the pearl
I'd never waste a wayward look again,
nor think to whistle at a pretty girl,
my senses finally curbed and turned within.
For nought can justify an outward glance
when but the merest part of gazing on
the inner light outshines all countenance!
No outer sun can match the inner dawn.
Its rising sweeps the shards into a gyre
of love beside which nothing can compete,
a peaceful storm consuming all desire,
a flame from which all worldly things retreat.
Lord, grant me grace to firmly hold the light
unto full measure in your perfect sight.

KLAMATH BASIN WRITERS

Kei Oni Garcia

GHOSTS

Do you think the other side is where all your past selves go?
Where they congregate
Cold mist that tingles on your skin? Or the other side of
soundproof glass in an interrogation room.
Talking to them is like a mirror
you look with empty eyes
because they're what Could Have Been.
They remind you that if you'd made different choices
maybe you'd be happier.
If only you'd said *no.*
You spray paint the glass black. Close and lock the
basement door with the word "regrets" scrawled on the
outside so that you know to not open it.
Ignore their wails at night, and try to carve something
better for your future. Light scares away the shadows. The
ones that drag you down into your own prison of missed
opportunities. You should have said no. But you didn't. So
your innocence is locked in the basement, killed and moved
over to a place you can't reach.

After three years of pretending and denial, one day they
break the lock.
To wander lost in your house. They stand at the foot of the
bed, and weep. Sometimes they go into the room next door
and scratch at the shared wall. The light of a phone screen
is the only thing you can see.
At some point you stop condemning them. There's a cold
key searing into your skin and you realize you're the one
that opened the door.
You missed them.

Why?

Why do you follow your ghosts?
What can they possibly tell you that would give you a sense
of purpose?

They fade through the drywall, a place you can't follow
them, unless you prefer your pain to seep through split
knuckles.
The bandages itch, and turn dark when your depression
iodizes in the open air of a lonely house.
You can hear their footsteps pace outside your door at night.
They shout and argue with each other sometimes, but you
can never make out what they say.
Sometimes in the morning when you stare into your cold
mug of coffee,
an apparition pulls up the chair across from you.
You try to make small talk.
All you hear is your own voice.
It crawls across your skin, and you hate the sound of it.
It makes you wish you'd never learned to speak.
Your voice: it's the thing that makes you unique, exclusive
to your own throat.
So why do sharp edges on a forgotten chalkboard sound
better?
Maybe that's the reason they won't talk to you.
Why they stare past you.
Why do you try to impress them? Maybe if you do, you'll
have something to look forward to when you join them.
Your hands shake. You scrape your nail over the half
removed "$3.00" paper sticker.
It won't come off.
You've only taken one drink, but that feels like far too
much already. When you can't take being ignored a moment
longer, you stand up. In a sudden way, that shatters the air.
The chair legs scream backwards over the kitchen floor
leaving permanent tracks. You scrub until your hands bleed
but they don't lift from the polished wood. Your mug tips
over, black coffee lays siege to your singular place mat.
The ghost only blinks. You make no effort to leave the
house in a hurry, because this is where you live, so what
would be the point.

You thought that you could collect their spirits in purple and blue Mason jars. The rust of the lids smells like blood on your fingers.

You never feel clean no matter how much water rushes over your skin.

It's impossible to recapture shapes.

There are regrets tugging at your arms when you walk the halls at night. You're not sure when you started doing it. But it's not like they disapprove. They don't feel much of anything. At least not when you look them in the face. They stare back, blank endless eyes. Just like they did on the other side.

You've tried it all. Being nice, screaming until your throat croaked. You've fallen to your knees and apologized, begged for them to give you anything.

You don't have a favorite. How could you?

They're all the same.

LUKEWARM

Waking up feels like being exhumed. She's always hated it, but he wakes up first and leaves a cold space in the bed every morning. He thinks she doesn't see the wistful look he gives her over his shoulder. The desolate sigh that ghosts through his lips just before he stands to leave.

The sheets pool like silk around his hips, bed bowed under his weight. Pale blue contrast with earthy skin.

She doesn't know what he wants from her. She remembers when they were new and their skin burned, she'd pull him back into bed and the air was warm and charged static. He'd smile against her skin, his brown eyes candle lit with love and desire.

All that romantic shit.

Now the window is left ajar, the curtains stir with icy exhales. Goosebumps rise over her skin. She tugs the blankets closer and forces herself back to sleep as he glides to the bathroom.

He used to be so solid. Now he's like mist. He drifts through the halls like an apparition. He leaves cold air rippling in his wake, the sheets feel like no one has ever occupied the space between the linen. His eyes never stay on her for long. Instead, they skate over her, water over lily pads. He doesn't meet her gaze anymore. Dour smoldering looks flick away just before she can really catch them. He looks at her like she's a monster.

She thinks that maybe she is.

Eggshells shattered over cold kitchen tiles. Black coffee, barely lukewarm from when he left early in the morning, tastes like nothing but sours her tongue all the same.

She leaves the house as cold and lifeless as it is when they get home.

He wakes when dawn is chilly and the sky mute.
Quiet, but there's a buzz in the air outside that reminds
him this is the time everyone is stirring, getting ready. That
energy ends at the front door, however. Inside is steeped in
an endless January morning.
He feels like he sleeps next to a corpse. Not a zombie,
because even they are driven by something. What he sleeps
next to is cold, unmoving. Her eyes are steely, rigid. They
don't have the soft give. He can see himself in the glassy
reflection, but it's not a mirror. Slowly the warmth faded.
The sun sunk behind her walls and refused to rise. It wasn't
fire and ice, meeting in the middle, creating flexible water
that filled their house. It was a bitter and cold wind that
whipped over his skin and left welts.
It extinguished him.
He looked at her, hoping for something. But, there was
nothing to find.
Not anymore.
He comes and goes, she doesn't notice. Old flames that offer
hope glow on his friend's list. Someone that could give him
something. But he refused to be the stereotype. A black
man still chasing tail, leaving his baby girl cold and alone.
His boys don't get it. Knows just what they'll say, words
he'll have to sift through the noise of a crowded bar to hear.
They'll call him a girl, a pussy. For wanting softness, and
validation.
He stays silent.
Life happens around him in glacial motion, and nothing he
does effects anything. His Mama stopped giving advice the
moment the choir filled the church with celebratory songs
of a life well lived. Said she was in "a better place now" and
a buncha other whack shit he wasn't sure he believed.
Because if it were true it wouldn't hurt so fucking bad.

It was cruel. No mom to see him off to college, to cry with
pride when he got his overpriced degree. Just a cold grey
hole in his heart.

The steering wheel was cold to the touch.
Like the bathtub filled with lukewarm blood,
stained porcelain. The white hollow door her
brother had punched a hole in to get it open.
The weight of caring for three kids alone must have
been too much for dear old dad.
That was okay though.
She told herself she was over it. Even though she stared at
the bathtub every morning with nothing in her eyes. She
pretended it didn't whisper to her.
She'd been better. Could smile over the numb ice in the
pit of her stomach. She could hide it even from herself
sometimes. She believed she was better.
But a certain fire that she took painstaking care to keep fed
was flickering out. The liquid of their relationship sizzled
over her skin, threw out hissing plumes of steam that
collected over the mirror in their bathroom. She'd clear
the condensation with a hand, rivulets of water dribbling
down over the crystalline surface, dropping to the cool
countertop. She tried to find her reflection, but couldn't.
She gave herself the same look he did.
Searching.
He wanted more than she could give. She was trying
though. Wanted to look at him and feel her heart jump
again.
She didn't know when it faded.

"Am I using him to fill the void?"
                    "Am I using her to fill the void?"
They ask themselves so often, it loses meaning.

NOSTALGIA

Nostalgia is a weird layering of feelings.
Disconcerting, but warm and familiar all the same.
But confusing.
Four walls that feel like home.
But not really.
Have you been here in a dream?
A past life maybe?
All you know is that it smells like the ticking
of a clock and tastes like memories on your tongue.
Longing for something you can't get back.
Because you never really had it.
You write again and again in stacked notebooks
"that's okay."
You might hurt for nothing.
But that's okay.
You want to go home.
That's okay.

Deep down we all want to go home.
Trouble is you haven't found it yet.
You try to imagine it, sleek counters
and lively house plants, with the smell of you
or someone you love embedded into the walls,
and dancing across sofa cushions.
It feels like contentment all wrapped up,
tangled in your throat, and leaving you
in tears because you can't find that place

All the others are cold. The walls harsh and
judgmental potted plants withering in the
back of your mind.

It's not home. The floors don't feel like
sunshine, or grass. The door isn't welcoming.
But that's okay.
You tell yourself.
Maybe one day.
Nostalgia for a place you've never been.

SOAK

Do you even feel the cold on your skin? Do
you hear the music around you? Pounding
against your ears like fists on a door.
Open up.
Cardboard boxes; moving is much more of
an end than a beginning.
Water dripping from a broken refrigerator.
Potting soil on white window sills.
How can you feel nothing, and everything
all in the same breath.
You ask yourself that every time you see
water drops roll down the shower walls.
The percentage on your phone ticks away
one by one but you left your charger, tied
around the wrists of your motivation,
in a ditch.

Nobody left flowers.
Nobody noticed she was gone.
You remember every time someone
hugs you.
And you feel empty.

There's permanent hair dye staining the
sink. You aren't going to clean it. What's the
point. It comes back every morning.
You remember every time you wash
your hands.
You remember every time the moon is on
your left side.
You remember every time the right song
comes up on shuffle.

Sing to anyone that will listen and tell
yourself that it helps. Look for yourself
inside of anyone that will look at you for
more than a second. Look away when you
remember you want to be invisible.
The thing about spilling makeup on a tiled
floor is that it's easily cleaned. It's not like
your emotions soaking into the floor.
Seeping into the walls, so that every once
in awhile you can see them at night. How
many good memories do you have to bathe
in to wash away all the evil ones. How long
till the sinewy corpses of your innocence
and wonder bury themselves in something
other than your mind?

Shampoo the floor as much as you'd like.
The bloodstain won't come out.

Liz Garcia

(Drawings in this section are by Liz Garcia)

THE LEPRECHAUN

The ghost of a chuckle
floatin' on the breeze
A flash of green and tan
out the corner of my eye
In a place, I am
where the trees are so old
and the glade well greened
with the glint of gold
It sparkles and shines
like a faerie dancing nigh

Is it possible, I ask…
A wee face appearin'
and, looking again
tis only a knothole I see
The grasses are swavin'
like someone's passin' by,
while my eyes are straying
caught up in the shadows
of birds flyin' high

The Leprechaun is playin'
in amongst the flowers
It was there…
Wasn't it?

LEAP INTO FLIGHT

Sometimes you just have to take a chance, take a leap, to move into a new phase of life. Otherwise, you can get stuck in your comfort zone. Trying out fresh ideas is a form of this, but a true leap involves the unknown. You must overcome your fears or discomfort, in order to take it.

Courage is found in facing up to our fears and doing something, even though we are afraid. Great growth occurs from taking such actions.

This kind of leaping puts one in mind of mountain goats, who leap up – down – and across – vertical chasms, landing on and leaping from, the tiniest of ledges. What kind of faith, do they possess?

The very act of leaping, involves leaving the earth, if only for a few seconds. Yet, in those seconds, we are flying. Spreading our metaphorical wings to cast off past burdens, we are released into a greater expression of who we are.

LISTENING

Sitting in a dappled glade
Elements of birdsong
animating the trees
Breathing the essence
of living earthiness
The freshness of green
is invigorating
I am at Peace
Listening
to the flowers grow

ON A FARAWAY HILL

On a faraway hill...
under the bright moon,
in a circle, they gather.
Lifting their voices
in the ancient song...
singing of joy
and of thanksgiving.
They learned it as pups,
from their fathers and mothers;
who mated for life...
to carry the pack forward
through the generations.
They sing in harmony,
some voices high...
and others pitched low.
On a faraway hill...
under the bright moon.

Klamath Basin Writers

Andie Icenbice

FREE BY THE END

I will journey through time and
I will walk between stars and
I will dance among gods and
I will sing within caverns deep in the earth.
I will swim in stardust and
I will be forged in dying starhearts and
I will sleep in the ocean depths and
I will listen to the stories of lone souls.
I will run through fields of wheat and
I will talk with the humans of old and
I will lament long lost ages and
I will paint echoes of the past on every rock and stone.
I will stand on the edge of space and
I will scream from the top of the world and
I will cry to fill forgotten rivers and
I will bury myself to feed the dying land.
I will live life as it is meant to be lived and
I will be free by the end of it.

MIDNIGHT SHOWER THOUGHTS

lately, i am not myself.
the mirror shows someone else's eyes, something unknown lurking in
their depths. the face looking back at me is a kindergarten craft mask, it doesn't fit. the voice
i hear is that of a stranger's, unfamiliar on my ears. the curves of my flesh are foreign to
me. i wear my body like a badly tailored suit. it feels wrong. my thoughts are not my own. the
people i coveted are slipping from my grasp, like a bad memory. i don't know them anymore.
my soul feels out of place, disconnected, unreal. i am not real. nothing is real. and yet
everything is. i feel like a ghost, as if my world is fake. the things out of my sight are blown away in
the wind, they fade from my mind. the places i've been no longer exist. places i will be are still
forming. something is wrong with me. i can feel it in the bones that are too big for my liking. my life feels
as though it is stolen, borrowed. i don't have much time. lately, i am not myself

A Sense of Unfairness

leftover dreams and checkered walls give you a sense of unfairness. doorless doorways leave you exposed to the world, thousands of eyes watching your every move. desktop disasters and decadent debacles are a spreading stain on your white polyester skin, uncapped and left for dead. thrown away like a torn bag, your only purpose in life unobtainable because the wolf's claws left reams in your skin and you can't hold anything in. planned communities of vacuum stripes fill you with a desire for perfection, creating an endemic of unsatisfaction in the city of your mind. they protest and they picket and they boycott and they riot until everything is perfect. everything is perfect. everything is perfect. everything. is perfect. except you. you're the red wine on the white silken couch, covered up and fruitlessly scrubbed. you don't do anything but irritate and annoy, embarrass and shame. you don't contribute anything to the discussion, but you're spoken of in frantic whispers and hushed tones. everyone sees you, but no one acknowledges you. you're there. but no one wants you to be. it all gives you a sense of unfairness.

DREAM

you see, he's always there. his face is always in the back of
my mind and he's hiding behind every corner just waiting,
waiting for me to make a mistake so he can take me back.
i have dreams about him. about going back to him after
this taste of freedom, the food i cook for him and i bland on
my tongue as i remember that feeling and wait days weeks
months years for my mother to come rescue me again.

it's like those nightmares when you're running as fast as
you can and you can see the door in front of you but no
matter how fast you run and how far you go it never gets
any closer and the thing behind you is always faster. i
wouldn't say he's my nightmare but when i dream of him i
wake up drenched in cold sweat with my heart in my throat
and fear in my eyes and despair in my lungs because dear
god i do not want to go back.

the medication keeps me from dreaming. when i pop those
little round pills i don't have to worry about seeing his face
in my dreams but a tiny voice in the back of my mind keeps
reminding me of the promise to never do drugs i made in
6th grade when that police officer came every week to talk
to our class. i promised him not to get addicted but how
was little me supposed to know that prescription pills were
the only way to stay sane?
take this but don't get dependent, my psychiatrist says. i

promise i won't but inside i'm screaming that these pills are the only way out and it's not my fault his voice yells at me in my head. you'd think i was crazy if i told you that. no, my father isn't back at his house, he's in my head and he's telling me i'm worthless. he's telling me i'm a problem and that no one loves me and that my girlfriend is cheating on me because i'm not enough and i never will be. because there's always someone prettier, smarter, funnier, stronger. someone who isn't stuck with demons on their shoulders, weighing them down so much that they collapse at your feet begging for sleep. because even in the place i should feel safest, he follows me.

it's not your voice, she says, don't listen to it. you see i've tried. i've tried so hard to not listen but it grates at my ears like rusty machinery and i can't help but hear when he screams at me to just do better. i know you can do better, he says. you're my child why aren't you good like me, why aren't you great like me why aren't you strong like me why are you just like your mother. why are you so weak he asks. why are you leaving why are you abandoning us think of your brother why are you leaving you're just like your mother. just like your sister.

just stop thinking about it, they say. but how can i stop thinking of missing doors and oven burns and gauze wrapped around my arms so i didn't bleed through my shirt at school? how can i forget about angry phone calls that make the office lady turn her cheek because she can hear what he says and she really can't find a pair of gloves to get dirty in? the late night talks with my sister that made me

78

think that maybe i could trust her when all she did was turn around and stick a knife between my 4th and 5th rib. they tell me to just get over it but i can't because he lives in my head and his lease isn't up til i'm dead.

just think positive thoughts, they say. but how can i think positive thoughts when my voice is just a whisper drowned out by his rage? he's taken over my mind and i'm not loud enough to post an eviction notice on his door. so all i'm asking is for you to talk a little louder. be a little nicer. love me a little longer. hold me in your arms. scream until i can't hear him anymore. please. i'm begging you. just help me be free.

That House

it does things to you, that house.

it has you trapped like a criminal and forced to repent for crimes you didn't commit and sins you're too poor to pay for. it has you in the confession booth with a gun to your head and a finger to its lips.

your tongue drips with defiance and your hairline with blood. they taste the same to you.

you're there again. a new face a new place a new town a new pace. but it's still the same. you're like a bird stuffed in a rusty wire cage that's much too small for your aching wings. your throat is hoarse and cold, the songs unable to escape any longer.

that house. it does things to you. it saps your life, it puts stale words in your mouth that don't fit your tongue and press against the insides of your teeth like bad braces. it forces your head down in compliance with threats and a grotesque smile. you hide yourself away in hopes that it'll leave you alone. but it never does. it watches over your shoulder, drooling judgment and whispering harsh words, only to deny those words ever being said when confronted by another. it's an incarnation of darkness, perched on your shoulder and looming over your head, with laughing eyes and sharp claws pressed to your neck, promising punishment if you step out of line. you try so hard but it's never enough. you're never enough.

it does things to you, that house.

SECRETS

I know the sound of ravens wings.
Of universe-born secrets nestled within their midnight
feathers.
I hear the knowledge of ages past fluttering by on the wind.
Their calls mimic the sound of grief, of wonder, of
things gained and lost, of words half forgotten and never
remembered.

I know the sound of ravens wings.
Of adoration whispered only when the sun claws its way
above the distant mountains.
Exchanges between lovers on pillows still warm with peace
and sheets still tangled with affection.
The wistful sighs and soft murmurs still remain buried in
the walls even after the sheets have righted themselves and
the left pillow grows cold again.

I know the sound of ravens wings.
Of words never spoken and regrets never erased.
The flames of guilt licking the insides of your mind and
leaving nothing around you but the charred remains of
a home you will never get back,
a life you always took for granted,
a family forever shattered
by the secrets hidden within the raven's wings.

HIM

there are roses blooming beneath your skin. they mark a
trail from just under your jaw to meander down your chest
and you wonder what treasure they could possibly lead to.

(they don't.)

you can feel their thorns pierce your lungs and the vines
wrap around your heart, squeezing as you try to restrain
your affections.

(you can't.)

you know their leaves block your airways and slice through
your words every time he so much as looks your way. he
leaves you speechless in your awe and you can hear the
titter of petals laughing at your hopefulness.

(you still wish.)

roots dig into your stomach and twist around your insides
until you're all but rearranged and you can't find it within
yourself to feel regret. you tell yourself it feels better this
way. you try hard not to remind yourself you're lying.

(you are.)

because he can't-
he couldn't possibly-
there's no way-

(he does.)

there are roses blooming beneath your skin. they mark a
trail from just below your jaw to disappear, hidden under
your collar. you know what treasure they lead to.

(his love.)
(his heart.)
(his soul.)
(him.)

KLAMATH BASIN WRITERS

Jo Johnston

WORDS

I know the feel of words,

words, like *maudlin*, feels
like a fat marshmallow filling
your cheeks, or like a lazy yawn;

or like the grating feel of grinding teeth
when speaking the word *grit*.

Sweet is a sensual word kissed from lips
that *pout* when articulating that verb,
or *tremble* with activity when uttering it.

Mother feels soft, secure, and safe, but
Daddy is filled with a playful spirit.

Romance is annunciated sensually;
lips out, then back—a courtship, just as
you reaches out and *me* pulls back,

like *sex*, brief and to the point, but
making love lingers on the lips and tongue.

Do you not feel *gut-wrenching anguish*,
as vividly as *light-hearted joy*?

DISAPPEARANCE OF AMELIA

Amelia has been missing since last Wednesday night—the night she told us of her unusual find. Out of concern I went to her house and knocked. No answer. I tried the door and found it was not locked. Lights were on in several rooms and the radio was playing somewhere. I called her name as I wandered from room to room but there was no response. Everything seemed to be in order.

I entered the kitchen last. It was in the back of the house with windows looking out over the yard where she had made her find. She was nowhere inside or outside. On the table was the radio playing western music, a half eaten bran muffin on a Wedgewood saucer, a teabag drenched in a blue mug of cold water—and the geode.

A huge magnifying glass, like one used by someone accustomed to doing dainty needle projects, was propped against the exposed end of the rock, as if someone had been using it to examine the exquisite crystals inside.

Something drew me to the stone. I sat in the chair where she had obviously been sitting and pulled it and the glass to me. I caught my breath in wonder as I peered into the depths of the magical cavern filled with sparkling multi-faceted crystal.

A narrow line, like a garden path, ran from the front edge of the stone and wound carefully among the spires and pinnacles of opalescence to finally disappear in the dark recesses at its depth. I was drawn into the heart of the rock. I saw each crystalline spike as individual, separate, isolated, yet an integral part of the whole, like a single angel in a choir of heavenly hosts.

I wandered among the peaks, delighting at a ray of light forming an almost-living beacon from one peak to another, threads of purple, violet, blue, gracing rainbows of red, orange, yellow, green. I felt the throb of the cosmos strobing in this inner space, heard filmy waves of music floating across fields of icy quartz. A scent of sweet vanilla or gardenia hovered faintly. The taste of cool minerals was on my lip.

I searched the depths, searching for something—I had forgotten what.

Then, deep in the shadows, for just a brief moment, I thought I saw movement, like someone in a red dress walking along a garden path, a basket filled with daisies over one arm. Amelia?

SUNSET SWEET SHOPPE

Somewhere,
    just beyond the rainbow,
        a sunset confectionery tests its recipes.

Yesterevening
    wispy threads of
        pink cotton candy spun
            so thin one could see peppermint swirls

floating in caramel sauce.
    Marshmallow clouds
        yield to velvety orange sherbet,
            then to plump raisins in whipped cream.

This evening
    soft lemon meringue pie,
        shades to fluffy apricot chiffon,
            succumbs to raspberry parfait,

deepens to purple plum pudding.
    Cinnamon candy apples
        guard butterscotch etched licorice boats
            sailing into pools of blueberry tarts.

COTTONWOOD'S STORY

I see the big truck with a boom coming up the road. It stops just outside the fence. Two men jump out and girdle my expanse with a tape.

I knew this day would have to come. I've grown too large for this small yard, and my age of 140 years makes the people in the house and neighborhood nervous that a severe storm may topple me into the house or road.

I was planted during the time the big two-story house, then known as the Beehive Hotel, was being built. It served this small community in that capacity for many years, until the first private homeowner, George Schofield and his wife and family took it over.

George's grown son, Lester, with his wife, Helen and their young family moved in a few years later. Lester's young son, Freeman, and his two sisters played as children in the shade of my maturing branches.

I fondly recall the day when Freeman proposed marriage to Hattie, the girl next door, as they sat under my spring green limbs.

A few years later, Freeman's and Hattie's daring little tomboy daughter, Jo, often climbed as high into my branches as possible. I recall how she would sit on one of the lower branches, her back pressed against my truck, as she read book after book during the long school breaks. She sometimes taunted her older brother into trying to climb up as high as she could, but he would always find excuses to go back to the ground.

Several years later I was the backdrop for photos of Jo holding her first-born daughter—standing alongside the child's great grandmother Helen, who had called this home.

* * * * *

The sound of the chainsaw is bittersweet in my hearing, as the teeth begin to chew into my side.

My time is ending. I've lived a good long healthy and fulfilling life. In truth, I'm not sad all of it is over; I am filled with gladness that it was.

THE OLD HOUSE

A couple miles from my grandparent's ranch house was their original homestead.

I was probably ten the first time I was actually in the empty, two-room house, sitting on a slight hill overlooking the hayfields flowing away to the south and west.

It had been a number of years since my mother and father had taken the time to visit it, and on this day Mom seemed to enjoy reminiscing about the "old days."

"Over there was the chicken house," she said, pointing. "One day my little brother, Jim went missing and we all looked for him, ever fearful that he'd gone to the creek by himself and had fallen in and drowned. But, after an hour or so, he came, sleepy-eyed, out of the hen house."

After she walked around the now-bare kitchen, Mom recalled the birth and subsequent death of three of her siblings—babies born in quick succession. They died, we now know, as the result of being RH factor babies.

"I wasn't told what was going on," Mom said. "They just didn't talk about anything so personal as pregnancy. But, I remember being awakened one night by sounds in the kitchen. I got up and peeked around the bedroom door. I can still picture Daddy sitting in front of the oven door, rubbing the body of a newborn boy, and saying 'Come on, little guy. Live. Live.'"

I tried to imagine the obvious grief of her mother, that pioneer woman, living away from any family or friends, other than her gruff-spoken husband.

In the house it was easy to imagine the old Hoosier, which now stands in my kitchen, with the flour sifter bin on one end and the sugar drawer on the other. I could easily imagine my grandmother rolling out biscuit dough on the pullout table.

As I think back to that day, all those years ago, when I visited that lonely, empty little house, miles from the nearest neighbor, I feel a pang of nostalgia and love for my quiet old grandmother with eyes the color of sky.

LOVABLES

My stepdaughter, Bonnie recently posted a lovely message on Facebook early one morning:

"Every morning a certain little girl's alarm beeps for five minutes or so, and then I have to go into the sea of pink, turn it off, move the blanket tornado, toss stuffed animals (and nine-times-out-of-ten, a book) aside, and crawl under the covers to snuggle. This is her request, and if she doesn't get her 'morning snuggles,' she has an almost impossible time of getting moving. It's so sweet, and taking five or ten minutes to do this has solved the past struggle of almost being late, and the stress of running behind. She's ten. I wonder how much longer this will be wanted... needed.... And, who's more spoiled? Me or her?!"

When I read it to her father, I heard a little catch in his throat, as a single tear formed in my own eye.

I have four daughters of my own, so I could relate to the sentiment, but I couldn't recall a moment quite like this in our household while they were growing up that had become a ritual.

I love my girls as much as Bonnie does Elaina, but our mornings were, "Hurry up...get dressed...eat, eat, eat.... where's your homework...get going... or we'll all be late."

All four turned out well, in spite of all that, and I doubt any of them would say they'd missed a morning snuggle with Mom.

But, if I could do it over again....? Maybe I'd have done something like Bonnie and Elaina more often.

My comfort is in recalling each of my daughters, in turn—singly, at one time or another—saying something like: "Someday, I want to be just like you, Mom."

Now I look at each of them, at the amazing adult women and see what they have become. And, I think, "I hope to be just like you, one day."

Klamath Basin Writers

Ken Johnston

IF TEACUPS COULD TALK

They would recall the
wonderful times we've shared
And mention the warmth
of your smile and sparkle in your eyes.

They would remind you of my skills,
my strength, and how much I care.
And they would rekindle the thoughts
that open your heart to me.

They would whisper secrets of
intimacies with bodies bared
And of dreams of the future
waiting to be realized.

They would tell of the beauty
and fastness of canyons colored red
or reveal paragons of emotional feelings
experienced in Pyrenees mountain retreats.

They would beg forgiveness
and plead for compassion
and promise improvement,
devotion, and commitment in return.

Yes, If Teacups Could Talk,

They would express how wrong, how unfair,
and how lacking of due process the past can be;
But they would convey to you how strong, how right,
and how lasting our future should be.

Or They Might Just Say I Love You.

Eclectic Voices from the Basin

An Inversion in Time

It's been ages since we left the canyon rim.
Four hours and countless jolts and jars and downsteps;
traversing downward in time past
layer upon layer of sandstone, schist,
and metamorphic records of the ages,
epochs, and eras to the river, the arterial life blood
and pulse of the canyon.
The river—the pulse of the canyon
beats through the seasons, the centuries.
It carries seaward the rock and its recordings.

We cross the bridge, tired, stiff, sore,
and consumed with the present.
We look down at the current
cutting still further into the past.
The river of now cutting the oldest rock of record
and the awareness that the river of the future
will cut further into the past
exposing millions to billions of years of geologic time.

I wonder—will infinite future
expose an infinite past?
Are there limits?
We are aware of our limits: painfully
and yet optimistically aware of our limits.
Or are we?
As the present segues into the future,
does it lengthen the infinity of the past?
Does it shorten the infinity of the hereafter?
Does the river have limits?
Does the future or the past have limits?
Are there limits?

I look down and ask the river.
Perhaps that is why we came down to this place
where the future meets the past at the NOW....

THE LAND OF BEYOND

Come, I'll take you to
the Land of Beyond
Where the Mountains are high,
and the Valleys are wide.

Where the skies are blue,
and the Rivers run deep,
And where the Trail is never
too long or too steep.

Follow me to the Land of Beyond;
over the Hill and through the Vale
Beyond still waters and down Rivers swift,
With Canoe and Paddle, or Saddle and Pack,
We'll travel the Trail and follow the Track

To the Land of Beyond.
Yes, come with Me to
the Land of Beyond,
And I'll show you where the Lingam meets
the Yoni at the Shakti

In the Land of Counterpane.
We'll enjoy the pleasures
And probe the Mysteries
In the Land of Beyond.

EPHEMERALITY

King Solomon said: *As for man, his days are as grass. As a flower of the fields, so he flourisheth. For the wind passeth over it, and it is gone, and the place thereof shall know it no more.*

Now that's Ephemerality!

I awoke in the vastness of the Black Rock Desert where twelve million years ago Sequoias towered in forests. Later, Pleistocene mammals—mastodons, camels, giant ground sloths—roamed the earth. Paleo Indians hunted some of them on the shores of Lake Lahontan.

Lake Lahontan yielded to "climate change" 12,000 years ago. Its five hundred foot depth and 8,600 square mile surface evaporated, leaving the playa I camped on last night.

I found a projectile point on the ground, and wondered which was more significant: the man who shaped it, hunted with it, and lost it, or the obsidian stone it was shaped from. The man had plans, skills, hopes, and a life, but the wind passed over it and he was gone. The stone remains into the future.

The little pleasures we feel—the hopes and dreams—come and pass. All are ephemeral in the infinity of time past and time into the future.

Ephemerality is reality in the everlasting vastness of infinity.

As a flower, so we flourish. But let us leave a sign—a projectile point. The place shall know us for it.

Klamath Basin Writers

Snowshoeing Through Lassen's Volcanic Wonderland

Darkness was rapidly encompassing us as a full moon rose above the stark winter profile of Lassen Peak, and the thought of an emergency bivouac was strongly unappealing.

I heard Hank stop to adjust a troublesome ski and knew that he, too, was worried we may not find the Summit Lake Cabin, which was quietly obscured under the winter snowpack.

"Here's the road," shouted Dale. "It can't be far now!"

I realized there had really been no cause to worry; we were all experienced at winter camping and had brought a small tent in case of emergency. But thoughts of finding the cabin with its roominess and hospitality encouraged us.

My three companions and I were familiar with the backcountry of Lassen National Park, but we shared a curiosity about its winter aspects. Our trek aimed to explore the potential this great preserve held for off-season visitors.

In retrospect, our journey began from Park Headquarters at Mineral, California. Having completed a ten-mile drive to the Winter Sports Chalet near the south park entrance, we unloaded the cars, adjusted our equipment, and signed out with the rangers on duty.

One of the rangers was preparing to lead a guided hike on snowshoes (furnished by the Park Service free) to Sulphur Works, an area of hydrothermal activity we would soon pass by. He kidded Hank Warren, a park naturalist and our guide, about fresh tracks of Big Foot, an ape-like man reportedly living in the Pacific Northwest, being sighted and reported by park visitors who mysteriously never returned!

100

We started out by dodging skiers on the congested slopes, a contrast to the uninhabited backcountry we would soon enter. In a few minutes we reached Sulphur Works where the "rotten egg" smell of Hydrogen Sulfide gases escaping from steam vents aggravated the difficulty of breathing the thin crisp high-altitude air.

Hank told us we were in the crater of an ancient volcano, named Mt Tehama, which once stood 11,000 feet in altitude, but during a cataclysmic upheaval, 2,000 feet of the top of the mountain had caved within itself, forming a large caldera similar to Crater Lake in Oregon. Ponderous ice age glaciers then tore out the sides of Tehama, leaving Broke-off Mountain, Mount Conard, and Mount Diller as remnants of the ancient rim.

Dave Rainey and I were wearing snowshoes and the going up was easier for us than for Hank and Dale, who were wearing skis. When we got to Emerald Point, we were surprised to find to find the park road completely obliterated. The slope which it crossed was so steep we were in danger of sliding 500 feet to the canyon floor. We removed our snowshoes and skis and took turns kicking footsteps in the icy crust. Ski poles helped us maintain our balance, but blustery winter winds slowed our progress.

After a quarter mile of tedious trail breaking, we completed our traverse of the steep slope. As we were refitting our equipment, Hank discovered that the toe piece to his binding had disappeared. After retracing his steps across the slope, he was still unable to find the missing part, and some time was lost jury-rigging his ski.

Traveling was easier as we reached Helen Lake, a deep glacial lake at the foot of Lassen Peak. Just two weeks before, there had been several different groups, totaling about eighty skiers and snowshoers camped there with hopes of climbing the ermine-robed volcano. Others had hiked one and half miles into Bumpass Hell, a miniature Yellowstone with ten acres of violently steaming fumaroles, boiling pools, and bubbling mud pots—a Dantean inferno—where steam rose from the warm lakes and pools in stark contrast to forty-foot snowdrifts nearby!

In summer, thousands of visitors walked down the trail, which is shaded by mountain hemlocks and affords spectacular views of the volcanic landscape, to visit this geothermal wonder. It was named after Kendall Vanhook Bumpass, an early prospector who hoped to mine sulphur in the area. A newspaper reporter persuaded Bumpass to guide him to the area.

While they were walking through it, Bumpass broke through a thin crust of earth and plunged his leg into boiling water. Some say that he then quietly walked into a snowbank to cool his leg. Others say a black cloud of blasphemy rose over his head that day. At any rate, legend says Bumpass later lost his leg due to the incident, and the reporter named the area Bumpass Hell.

The snow depth averaged seventeen feet as we crossed the summit of the pass. Hank pointed out two small moraines on the eastern flanks of Lassen Peak that were remnants of the last Ice Age, which ended about 10,000 years ago, indicating that Lassen Peak, perhaps the world's largest plug dome volcano, rose rapidly 2,500 feet above its base about 11,000 years ago.

"Just imagine the tremendous earth-shaking pressures that forced up a cubic mile of rock through the earth's crust!" Hank exclaimed.

Dropping in elevation, we passed Cliff, Shadow, and Terrace Lakes, all blanketed deeply by snow. As we entered an open forest of giant red fir, my mind floated lazily along with the rhythmic sounds of snowshoes softly breaking the crust.

Suddenly, I snapped out of my reverie as Dale Wilson schussed past, uttering a Tyrolean yodel amidst a storm of flying powdery snow. Dave and I now envied the skiers who in turn envied us on the ascent.

Evening was approaching, and anticipation of reaching warmth and security of a roomy cabin grew as we neared Summit Lake. But we were surprised at how twelve feet of snow could obscure familiar landmarks and change the appearance of the landscape. Shadows were lengthening and more light seemed to be coming from the snow than from the sky above, contributing to disorientation as we searched for clues to where the cabin was located.

Then someone found a large pillow of snow that marked the cabin's location. Hank crawled down a tunnel to remove a padlock from the window, but he discovered that his keys were not in his pocket.

Our hearts sank as our thoughts again turned to spending the night cramped up in a tiny tent. A frantic and rather thorough search of Hank's pack revealed the keys, which had been secluded in a "safe place"!

The glow of a Coleman lantern soon warmed our hearts as the water from melting snow began to boil. Coffechino, a mocha drink made of coffee, cocoa, sugar, powdered milk, and melted marshmallows, whetted our appetites as freeze-dried stew simmered on the small Optimus stove. Dinner was concluded with a dessert of chocolate pudding topped with a handful of "Gorp," a high-energy combination of chocolate candies, peanuts, raisins, coconut, cornflakes, etc.

After dinner conversation segued into a short session of stories about past adventures and dreams of future explorations before our thoughts turned to sleep. Beds had to be lowered from "rodent proof" wires suspended from rafters. I poured some hot "melted snow" into my canteen and placed it at the foot of my sleeping bag to keep it from freezing during the night and doubled as a hot water bottle. With toasty feet, I drifted off to sleep.

When morning came, I was awakened by a delicate ray of light that somehow found its way through deep blanketing snowdrifts and shuttered windows. I slowly became aware of the overwhelming sound of silence, a silence so pure my ears ached with the strain of trying to hear a sound, detecting only the rhythmic pulse of my heartbeats.

I must have drifted off to sleep again because soon I heard the rattle of pans and the hiss of the tiny Optimus stove as Dale and Dave prepared breakfast. After a hearty meal of freeze-dried cheese omelet reconstituted with water, hot chocolate, and a can of crushed pineapple—a luxury found in the cupboard of the cabin—we policed the cabin, resuspended the bunks, swept out tracked-in snow, and reloaded our packs.

Each of us carried the necessities for winter survival: a down sleeping bag, Ensolite pad, waterproof tarp, food, and warm clothing. In addition to this, Dale carried the small emergency tent we had disdained last night.

Dale commented about the pack's weight as he handed it out the window and up the snow tunnel to me. "It feels like a baby grand piano with shoulder straps." I agreed.

I walked a few yards out into the meadow in search of the stream that so peacefully meanders through acres of wild flowers in the summer, and found it at the bottom of a steep canyon of snow. Several rainbow trout were disturbed by my intrusion and darted into deeper pools of crystal clear water.

Looking up I saw Lassen Peak, stark and white against a background of blue, a portrait of tranquility. What a contrast to the violence it unleashed on May 19, 1915 when molten lava spilled over the crater rim, melting the spring snowpack, creating a tremendous mud side, killing everything in its path. Then for three days, pressures built up within the

mountain until a violent blast of atomic proportions tore out the top of the mountain, sending a tephra cloud of rock, ash and debris to an elevation of 30,000 feet. So much debris was extruded that an inch of ash settled on the streets of Reno, Nevada, over 100 miles away.

Returning to the cabin, I slung on my pack and joined the others as we strung out single file to cross the frozen and deeply blanketed surface of Summit Lake. We wondered how it could be so hot in winter as we laboriously worked our way up the ridge near the base of Hat Mountain, an ancient cinder cone volcano.

Looking eastward from the ridge, we saw a series of cinder cones, the most recent of which erupted as late as 1850 and was observed by early pioneers in the area. Near its base is the Nobles Emigrant Trail, which many of California's ancestors traveled.

Hank added that the Cinder Cone, along with Lassen Peak, were set aside as national monuments on May 6, 1907 by President Theodore Roosevelt. They were later incorporated into a national park on August 9, 1916, to be preserved "for all people to enjoy forever."

We found that the snow didn't quench our thirst, and by noon we were glad to stop and light our tiny stoves to melt snow for tea and hot chocolate. Perched on our packs, we ate a lunch of crackers, cheese, sausage, and dried fruit. Dave then shared a tin of smoked oysters and baby clams with all of us, except Hank, who claimed he had suddenly become a vegetarian!

Refreshed and rested, we donned our packs and dropped from the ridge to upper Grassy Swale, where the tiny insectivorous sundew plant blooms all summer and where we now saw the tracks of a coyote wandering in search of food.

Suddenly, I heard the sharp, resounding crack of a twig. My mind flashed to the reality that all twigs are deeply

105

buried, and also that our destination still lay 20 snow-covered miles from here. I lifted my foot and the snowshoe drooped like a wilted flower from my boot.

In winter travel, where a small factor can mean the difference between life and death, one man's problem becomes every man's problem. Dave and Hank immediately cut fir saplings for splints while Dale converted his "baby grand" pack into an emergency workshop.

Using miniature pliers and a roll of high tensile bailing wire and the sapling branches, Dale soon cured the "lame" snowshoe. Although heavier and more prone to pick up compacted snow, it would prove quite serviceable for the rest of the journey.

In the summer, Lassen's 160 square miles of back country is crisscrossed with 150 miles of well-marked trails. But in winter, a topographical map and compass are essential to hinterland travel.

Even with these navigational aids, we missed the upper arm of Horseshoe Lake and emerged from the forest on the lower arm. No one complained of the extra distance, because ahead lay a most breathtaking tableau of unblemished white expanse framed with mountains and conifers.

Overhead the blue skies gave way to darkening clouds that eclipsed the sun to produce a tremendous rainbow-like corona. We wondered if this was foretelling an impending storm, but as we dropped from the last ridge toward Juniper Lake, the clouds opened up and allowed the rays of the setting sun to paint their tufted forms with hues of salmon, saffron, and yellow in a sapphire sky.

The tiny cabin, called the Juniper Lake Hilton, proved as hospitable as its namesake. Soon our tired muscles and the soporific warmth of the fire sent us dreaming.

When we awakened in the morning, we discovered

that the windows and door of our tiny castle were covered with a kaleidoscopic pattern of ice crystals, reminding us of a winter scene in the Dr. Zhivago movie.

We stepped outside and the brilliant sunlight reflected by the vast whiteness was blinding. Donning sunglasses and packs, we began the last leg of our trek. Soon we crossed a stream high-shouldered with snow and bordered with aspen, alder, and cottonwood trees. We stopped to investigate the wintery elegy of a Douglas squirrel portrayed by tracks ending suddenly in a death scenario marked by the violence of an owl's wingbeats imprinted in the snow, vividly punctuated by a tinge of blood and a vestige of fur.

For several moments we contemplated the stark reality that life is too short to waste any part of it, and we struck out again for our destination with new resolution.

The remaining miles stretched out endlessly, but were suddenly ended as we reached the mountain town of Chester. Raedell Warren, Hank's wife, was waiting to drive us to the Timber House Lodge where we feasted on veal cordon bleu in the warmth of a candlelight decor. Piano and organ music set the mood, but our minds stayed tuned to the joys of the wilderness.

Klamath Basin Writers

Leigh M. Lane

RE: HOME

Sharon's limbs went weak at the sound of fists on nearby doorways, the footfall closing in. Even expecting the noise, she jumped when the frantic knocking rattled her door, and her lungs went heavy as she rushed to gather what she could carry.

She paused at the end of the hallway, adjusting and rearranging a cumbersome load of bags and rolling luggage.

"Andy!"

"Yeah, I heard 'em." He came up the hall with three bags of his own.

She motioned toward a backpack sitting near her feet. "It's too heavy. Could you get this one, please?"

"Can you leave it? I'm about at capacity."

"It's our *food*."

He exhaled deeply. "Carry my clothes?"

She nodded, and he handed over one of his bags. She took it begrudgingly, and he heaved the heavy backpack over one shoulder. The added weight of the clothes triggered something in her on an emotional level, and she fought a new onset of tears.

She turned before he could see the struggle on her face. "I guess this is it."

"Yep." He began toward the door, brushing gently past her.

"Think we'll be back?"

"I hope so," he said.

With one last good look at her beautiful home, a knot growing tight in her throat, she followed Andy to the door. The sense of dread that had been roiling through the

core of her body suddenly took on a whole new somatic level, and for a moment she thought she might vomit. Taking a few deep breaths, she leaned against the wall and collected herself.

As the door opened, the sounds of grief and panic spilled in. The young couple watched for a moment, taking in the chaos, when an officer motioned for them to remember their masks. The two exchanged relieved glances and ducked back in long enough to each grab a mask and a jacket from the utility closet. Sharon's thoughts were a jumble, and she felt certain they were forgetting something important, but there was nothing to be done about it now. Andy locked the front door.

As though it mattered.

Sharon pulled close to her husband, staying right with him while they hurried toward the stairwell. While she recognized most of the faces lining up to exit the building, they all seemed so foreign to her. Maybe it was the anguished looks that made them all appear so different, or maybe the confusion of the moment had her too overwhelmed even to process a familiar face. She made eye contact with someone, but only for a second, and then each turned away without any further acknowledgment.

They fell into a line when they reached the stairwell. While they didn't come to a complete standstill, they descended the stairs slowly. The air had become acrid and uncomfortably warm from the number of anxious bodies filing through, and the din of voices trying to speak over one another made the narrow passage feel even tighter than it was. Sharon struggled to breathe, as though the air itself had become too thin to sustain everyone inside.

They only had a few flights to descend, but each step came at a crawl. An outburst one floor down reduced that to a halt. A middle-aged woman had turned around, and now fought against the crowd to return upstairs, dragging her teenaged daughter with her. Rings of sweat saturated the woman's shirt, and her eyes were wide and beady with panic. The girl with her looked around absently, too confused to have an opinion.

"What's your problem, lady?" a short, stocky man snapped as she lunged past.

"Not going out there," the woman muttered. "Nope, we're not going."

She knocked into an elderly woman, nearly throwing her backward off her step. The older woman shrieked as though she'd been assaulted, and the young man beside her sprang between them.

He shifted his weight, leaning in until his face nearly met hers. "What's your problem?"

"Nothing! And I didn't hurt her—"

"How about I shove *you* down the stairs?"

"Just trying to get back to my floor," said the woman.

The man scoffed. "This is an evacuation, lady. You stay, you die." He shoved past her, and he and the older woman continued their slow descent.

Others followed their lead, rudely pushing past the middle-aged woman and her daughter, who now looked ready to cry. Still, the two fought their way up the steps, somehow making room where there was none despite the thick line of people moving against them. The speaking volume rose, making hearing any one individual close to impossible, although Sharon could tell by the tones of voices that most of them were giving the woman hell for holding up the line.

The woman managed to yell loudly enough for her voice just to overpower the rest, "What if the rumors are true?"

Her question did nothing to alter the overall tone throughout the stairwell, but it did make Sharon feel less secure about what they were doing. She'd personally questioned the reports. While their air quality was definitely on the hazardous side, she knew people who lived in cities that were far worse. The water reports had thrown her most. Sharon had never noticed anything wrong with their tap water. Granted, she bought the most expensive filters, but if that made a difference, why not just make sure everyone had good filters? Why displace a whole city? Wasn't the whole world just as polluted?

Could it be possible that the rich actually were paying to have the working class moved out of the better-kept areas? Would money claim what little good was left of this world?

Would the water in their new home run as clear? Or might even the worst of the rumors be true?

Sharon dismissed the thought with a frantic shake of the head. No, this move was for their own good. She couldn't give in to the alarmists. She'd seen the discord those people seemed to get off on stirring, the misinformation they'd so subtly filtered into the mainstream ear too many times. These things simply happened; there was no nefarious force behind this move.

The middle-aged woman and her daughter finally came upon Sharon and Andy, who did nothing to add to their misery, but also did nothing to aid them along. As soon as the young couple cleared the minor roadblock, their pace resumed its steady crawl.

Sharon let out a nervous laugh. "Wow, what a loon!"

Andy didn't seem to hear her, and she let it go. How anyone could hold any kind of conversation in this place was beyond her. The sound seemed to amplify the farther down they moved, with only stray words clearing the mess of otherwise meaningless noise. The sound felt nearly palpable, permeating Sharon's body and competing against her for the surrounding air.

Andy leaned in to say something, but his words also dissolved into the commotion. Sharon pointed to her ear and shook her head. He moved his lips to her ear, and she felt the warmth of his breath brush past her when he repeated himself: "Looking forward to having cable TV again—just like all the rich people!"

The thought excited Sharon, and she nodded.

Then she had to wonder if she actually believed it. Was it even possible for a place to have those kinds of resources? And then to allocate those resources to something so frivolous as television for all... the more she thought about it, the more ridiculous it became. She couldn't think of one person she was still in communication with who still had TV in their sector. They were being driven, rounded up, guided by promises too beautiful to refuse.

Her muscles going tight, she clutched onto Andy's hand. "I don't want to go."

He turned with a concerned glance when the next step down opened up and she refused to take it. When she still didn't move, he gave her a gentle tug. She shook her head.

He forcibly moved her to his side when the protests began, and then she tugged at him until he leaned close enough for her to scream into his ear.

"I want to go back home," she tried. "Please, Andy!"

He responded with a confused face.

"Please, can we just go back home and talk about it?"

He moved to her ear. "Have you lost your mind?"

"It's too good to be true! Don't you see? The rumors weren't all false—"

He rolled his eyes and stood fully upright, putting

himself in spotty earshot. She tugged frantically, but he merely shook his head.

"Who do you know who has TV, not to mention enough power on their grid to allow *everyone* electricity twenty-four/seven? *And* they have fresh water?" She realized no one was listening—Andy wasn't even looking remotely at her—and she fell silent.

The line inched forward, and Andy coaxed her down another step. Tears streamed down her face, and she tried again to convince him to listen to her.

Another step down.

Hot, dizzying panic overtook her when she realized how close they were to the first-floor hallway. She pulled her hand free and tried to turn around, but Andy blocked her path. Desperate and out of ideas, she sucked in a deep breath and screamed her throat raw.

Silence.

Sharon stared up at her husband, but she hoped everyone else who could hear would also consider her words: "It's too good to be true. Something's not right. Please, let's go back."

No one said anything for a moment. Finally, a young man standing a flight above them yelled down, "Will you people move? We don't got all day."

The din of voices returned, and the shuffle downward and out to the hallway continued. Andy pushed Sharon out, but she ducked against the wall and yanked away her arm when he tried to pull her. The acoustics distributed the noise better there, and the couple was able to bicker it out without getting right into each other's ears.

"This is scary—I get that—but you need to get your head on straight, Sharon."

"But don't you see what's happening? No one has TV!"

"But we *will*! There are places that have all sorts of

115

things figured out. You'll see." He tried to pull her back into the line, but she squirmed from his grip.

"Then why not just make this place better? Why move?"

"You read the bulletin," he said, the impatience in his voice bordering on anger. "You know why we have to move. You're just nervous."

"But what if I'm right?"

"This is not the time to be losing it. We've got one ride to Capital City—*one ride*."

"But—"

"And then, this place becomes a ghost town, Sharon. No more food shipments. No more transport services. Nothing."

"But—"

"I'm not going to stay here and rot, and neither are you."

"But I don't want to die."

"You're being ridiculous." He shoved her back into line with intimidating force. "I'm not losing my wife to a bout of temporary insanity."

"Andy—"

The line filed toward the door leading outside, and Sharon found herself unable to fight her way back out.

Andy nudged her as they neared the door. "Put on your mask."

She shook her head.

"We're going out, Sharon."

"I'm not."

He tried to force the mask on her, but she fought it off. They reached the door, and she froze. The line kept moving despite her, and it only took the help of one other man to get Sharon—kicking and screaming—clear of the threshold. Someone else had her mask on her a moment later, and Andy expressed his thanks as those nearby pitched in to get the hysterical woman on the bus.

They put her in the back, blocked in by too many larger bodies to fight her way back off, and someone suggested they gag her when she refused to stop screaming. Andy covered her mouth, and her screams transformed into long, horrified sobs.

The bus filled, the doors shut, and the engine started.

"Please..." she shrieked through the tightly clasped hand.

Andy jerked her close, eyeing her as if she were an insolent child. "Knock it off! The other people in here want to ride in peace."

The two stared one another down.

"You're embarrassing yourself."

Sharon went quiet, and he released her. She turned and watched out the back window as the bus rolled forward. She labored her mind for some means of last-minute escape, but not one helpful idea came to mind. She was trapped. Nothing left to do now but wait.

They drove through half-real world or soot and shadow. Buildings shifted in and out of view, landmarks revealing themselves only to be swallowed moments later by the haze. The dark sky reflected thick, heavy air, and although they appeared to drive into a heavy fog, a hint of sepia betrayed that it was, in fact, either smoke or smog.

She sat in silence, watching her city dissolve into the obscure distance, and then she sat forward. Andy tried to talk to her, and she ignored him. She knew where they were headed.

And as soon as they reached the trains, so did everyone else.

THE END

KLAMATH BASIN WRITERS

Laura Larsen

MY LOVE AFFAIR WITH
THE LOS ANGELES TIMES

Despite numerous calls and letters asking us to subscribe to the *Los Angeles Times*, the result was always the same—the *Times* did not deliver to our rural canyon home at the far edge of Los Angeles County. They had failed to tell their marketing team.

During those years we had to sustain ourselves with the *Sunday Times* only, which we purchased at the grocery store on Saturday evening. The actual news wasn't as current as Sunday morning but the good parts were there—especially the *Home Magazine*. Ah, how I loved the color photos of gardens, recipes, and decorating schemes, many of which could be applied to our humble dwelling.

Finally, the *Times* agreed to deliver, but only to our mailbox, which was a half-mile up our dirt driveway. Rain or shine, we hiked up there before drinking coffee.

I moved to Klamath Falls, Oregon, and in addition to missing my friends and the ocean, I deeply missed *The Los Angeles Times* and my favorite columnists and sections. In addition to the national news, which didn't usually include hog prices and the upcoming potato festival parade that were featured in our new local newspaper, there were reviews of art, movies, and books. Even the obituaries were fascinating.

After complaining to my friend, Diane about the lack of stimulation in my new newspaper, she began mailing the good bits of the *Los Angeles Times* to me about once a month. Yeah, I know, I could have read it on line, but it is not the same. There was the ritual of spreading the paper out

on the kitchen table, the smell of the newsprint, and folding over pages to read later.

Once I settled in and found Klamath's more-than-fabulous library, and our local newspaper got new editors who spruced up its pages and helped me find my way around this new community, Diane started sending the packets every three to four months.

One such arrived today. In the Arts & Books section, I wasn't so fascinated by the cover article on the Coachella Music Festival, but just below, the headline read, "How can poetry help us talk about gun violence?" This led me to the back page, which described an event created by PEN America, of poets reading their works, followed by responses from activists. This event, I thought, was something we could repeat in Klamath Falls.

Below this story was a color photo of a long-haired, bearded man with large eyeglasses, standing chest-deep in a body of water, surrounded by stunning purple lotus blossoms. His book, *The Plant Messiah*, described the rarity of specific plants growing on the islands of Mauritius and Rodriguez, in the Indian Ocean. Now, where else would I have learned about this place and these plants, as well as the author, Carlos Magdelena?

Back to page six, I found an article showing photographs of HAPA, a Hawaiian word meaning *part*. The photographer, Kip Fullbeck, made portraits of subjects who were mixtures of Asian, American, European, and African ancestry. Fifteen years later, she re-shot the same subjects and placed the portraits next to the original prints. She noted that, statistically, in 2015, one in seven babies were multiracial, up 10% since 2000. It seemed a timely project given that some are trying to cleanse our country's people of color.

Across the centerfold was a review of the book, *Sharp: The Women Who Made an Art of Having an Opinion*, by

Michelle Dean. She compared and contrasted Nora Ephron, Dorothy Parker, Joan Didion, Pauline Kale, Susan Sontag, and Hannah Arendt. Even if I had not read the works of all of these women, I knew who they all were, probably from reading *The Los Angeles Times* most of my adult life. These authors wrote during the decades when women were being criticized for their intelligence, even while they were hired by high-end magazines, newspapers, and film companies.

At the bottom of the page was a summary of what could be enjoyed at the upcoming Los Angeles Festival of Books: panels and book signings from every genre, ethnic food, and live music. I had been present this event in the past. It was colorful, stimulating, and very well attended. I felt sad to miss this year's attractions.

All of the above and more was in the first section of Art & Books. I have yet to read two Calendar sections, in which movies, plays, and comedians are reviewed, and two California sections, to keep me apprised of the happenings in my birth state, the intriguing obituaries, as well as the good humor and kindness of the columnist, Steve Lopez.

Now with a week of promised warm days, I envision myself stretched out on my chaise lounge in my quieter town, but still soaking up the culture and creativity from the *LA Times*—the best of both worlds.

LOVE

The Beatles sing, *Love is All There Is*. Jerry Jampolsky writes *Love is Letting Go of Fear*. In the Bible, First Corinthians says Faith, Hope, and Love, but the greatest of these is Love. One of my favorite movies, *Love, Actually*, depicts all kinds of love, between all kinds of people.

It is also a word that we use loosely: "I love ice cream," or "love it or leave it," in a slangy fashion, or "don't ya just love it?" But what is love? An emotion? A thought? An idea? Does it tie everything together? Or drive us nuts as we yearn for this mysterious concept?

The first time I "fell in love," I was so swept away that on waving goodbye to my beloved, I walked smack into a cement pillar...good thing my head was turned toward him or my nose would have been broken. But was that love, or swept-away-ness?

In most Western countries, love is a prerequisite for marriage. In some Eastern countries, the parents, along with astrological aspects and finances, choose their child's spouse without the young couple ever having met.

Often, those in such an arrangement say they "grow to love each other." In *Fiddler on the Roof*, Tevye sings to his wife, "Do you love me?" while their children have begun to "choose their loves." She replies, "I wash your clothes, I cook your soup, what do you mean, 'do I love you?'"

123

I recently watched a Ted Talk called "Three Lessons of Revolutionary Love in a Time of Rage."

The speaker, Valerie Kaur, encouraged love of other, love of enemy, and love of self. It seemed timely advice for these days of separation from one another.

I feel that "love is" the combination of brother and sisterhood, kinship, affection, and caring...all are important qualities to practice, wherever love is found.

THE SEMINAL WEEKEND, 1981

It was the long weekend following Thanksgiving of 1981. The eight of us friends had all had the normal family dinners as usual on Thursday. The four couples ended up hanging out at our home for the rest of the weekend. Not everyone slept at our home but we regrouped every morning after breakfast. There were hikes, hot tubbing, more food, and lots of laughter.

Each of the couples had one successful creative person, and one seemingly not creative person. There was Carl, the potter and sculptor, and me; Bob, the published writer, and Judy; Victor, the published writer, and Barbara; and Linda, the actress and dancer acclaimed on both coasts, and Jim. The *non-creative* spouses functioned as support members for the artists: the promotion, the paperwork, the listening to new ideas, not to mention keeping their households running. Among us there were six young children, who cavorted happily throughout the house and yard during our gathering.

I had been having something burbling inside me for a long time, but didn't know what it was or what to call it. So, maybe it was me who instigated the huddle in the living room with the non-artists.

I shared that most recently, Carl and I had been hosting pottery sales. Often, I would hear someone say a version of, "Oh, you guys are *so* creative!" Without a moment's hesitation, I would respond, "Oh, not me, it's just him!" Or, someone might say, "I just can't draw a straight line," and I would follow with "Me either," as if drawing a straight line was the true way of knowing a creative being.

So, here we were, the four "non-successful-in-the-world" spouses, gathered around the fireplace on a cold November afternoon. It was too early for wine so our conversation had a serious tone.

I asked, "What's the deal here? Why are *they* producing

125

art and we are not? What is creativity? Were they born with it and we were not? Or were they nurtured to develop it and we were not? Was a product, such as a platter, a book, or a part in a play, the only measure of creativity? Why do we automatically help them with whatever they need, right now!?"

I was on a roll. These questions oozed from the muck and mire that swirled unnamed in my psyche.

Each of us was thoughtful for a while.

Judy said she was raising her children plus a special breed of dogs and didn't have time to think about being creative.

Jim was interested in making videos, but nothing had come of it so far.

Barbara had been immersed in the writing world, not only through her husband, but also via her father who was an editor at a large publishing house. She had worked there between college semesters but had never written herself.

And me? I was the quintessential Virgo homemaker, gardening, keeping our home pretty—if not all that clean—and being handmaiden for the great artiste!

There were some vague responses to my queries, but they were more like stirring the pot, than serving the meal.

For five years, we had a pottery boutique. Being there five days a week had shown me I had a knack for making a welcoming space and for being with people. Hardly an hour passed that someone wasn't sitting in the chair across from me, telling me a story or their troubles.

Then, Carl moved on to designing and building a narrow catamaran that was paddled like a kayak, and was more stable.

We closed the boutique. I was back on the mountain, weeding, making bread, and asking "how high" when told to jump. I had not considered that interaction with other people was a creative gift.

As we gathered around the long oak counter in the kitchen that evening to cut and chop turkey into quesadilla fillings, we were quiet outwardly, but the conversation had not left my mind.

My neighbor, Pola, had kindly taught me to make square, gold wire jewelry. I got proficient enough to sell it at the boutique, but I was pretty much copying what she taught me—I can't recall that I made my own original designs. I also made some porcelain picture frames while helping Carl in the studio. They sold at the boutique, but were kind of clumpy—the round openings not quite round, the rectangles often like squares or parallelograms. I was still looking for an art form, but I was definitely not a painter, potter, or a jeweler.

Once the first version of the Paddle Cats was completed and selling, I had no problem hoisting one above my head and charging through the surf to demonstrate their simplicity and lightweight to prospective clients. But that did not seem creative to me, just kind of gutsy.

After the Seminal Weekend, Barbara sent a watercolor of my front porch and a poem:
To let you know we enjoyed your salon,
With writers and artists, actors, and moms

Your home is enchanting, the food divine,
Not to mention the four bottles of wine

The energy which flows through your front door and home
Is there, like your friends, for reasons well known

So just to say thank you, for letting us share,
Inspiring moments, with people who care

The poem and painting awakened me. I got an *ink*ling that I did have something to say, though what or how I had no idea.

127

We had purchased a Smith-Corona 2200 so I could make invoices for the Paddle Cats and do the bookkeeping, so maybe it would become a tool for my endeavors.

I had no spot of my own—and I had read about the importance of having that in Virginia Wolf's *A Room of One's Own*—another arrow in the target of my discontent.

Our closet was a multi-use room, as it housed our turntable and record collection, as well as our shoes and humble assortment of clothes, including my seventeen long skirts and Carl's rugged work clothes.

I cleared a stack of 33 rpm albums from one of the shelves. I placed the typewriter there, which I could use while standing up. I decided to start my first creative idea by interviewing Carlos, our friend from Chile, because his life, to me, had been so worldly. I knew nothing about interviewing, despite hours of listening to them on KPFK public radio while working in the studio.

Carlos was a willing subject and let me ask a series of questions I'd thought up. I returned to my closet-office and typed it up. I asked Carl, and my son Erik (who was now around twelve or thirteen), if they would listen to me read my first piece of creative writing.

They listened quietly. I finished. They remained quiet. One of them finally said something, and I know it was not critical or mean. But I could hear my own words out loud—it was clumsy and uninformative, despite the unique character of Carlos.

I turned away without saying anything and went into our room. I threw myself on the bed and started sobbing. *Where, oh where, and how will I find my creative gifts? My voice?*

It wasn't long before those questions began to be answered, but not in any way I had imagined.

Marie Lee

High Desert Cemetery in Autumn

I seldom find beauty as I drive by there
In the crackling and hot,
Summertime air.
But now, in mid-autumn, my glances see
Falling leaves.
Some are golden, and some are brown.
They sift through half barren branches
As they float to the ground.

Down to the ground where
the trees are rooted quite firm.
The grass, unlike tan brittle summer,
is once again green.
Green from the moisture stored in
Mother Earth's basin-like urn,
And sprinkled with dew
By nighttime nymphs
That human eye never has seen.

These days I find it a place of beauty and rest.
Grey granite headstones,
Some short, some tall,
Tell the story of how living man
Has carved out his best
To leave a marker that proves
Those bones made a difference,
No matter, no what,
As they lived mortal lives, after all.

I find a shade of relief to my soul
As I drive by that ground,
And notice the silent beauty around
That hallowed place,
Where the physical bones of those who begot my bones
Are buried deep in the ground.

It scares me not, and brings me peace
To know that someday I'll join them there,
When my body wears out and God's angels
Reach down to give me release,
And turn *my* soul loose
To drift off somewhere.

I'm doing the best that I know how to do
To tell the story of those who knew,
About the story of those who went on before.
I pray for those stories to open a door.

I want my children to know,
And pass on to their brood,
The story about their own special marrow,
And history of yore.

I pray as they happen to drive by that place,
Where my bones lie buried,
Peaceful and sound,
They'll see only the beauty and find certain peace
In the fall of the year,
As leaves,
Some golden, some brown,
Sift through half barren branches
As they float to the ground.

THE NEW COWHAND

A new cowhand's a comin' to the Lazy SC.
We don't know who it is jest yet;
We'll have t' wait an' see.
Will he give a hand at brandin'
Like his older brother, Jack,
Or will she twirl on dancin' toes,
Like her sister, Norah, has a knack?

All them there's questions,
Thet we don't know the answer to.
But, one thing's shore as mornin's comin',
We're not leanin' either way,
Pink or blue.

Some of us has been around,
For years thet we don't count.
We've rid the ol' SC ourselves,
On horses long wore out.
We've turned them out to pasture,
An' hung our saddles up.
But we still see them ridges,
An' smell the springtime sage.
'Cause the memory of the ol' SC
Hangs 'round us as we age.
An' we're thinkin' this new hand
Is gonna turn right out to be,
One more of us,
Who'll make some dust,
On trails thet we can't see.
Someday, a way off yonder,

132

A long way down the trail,
Fer thet new hand's a babe, ya know,
An' needs some time to play an' grow,
There'll come a time to stop, an' look, an' see,
What God, Hisself, placed 'round about,
An' left the ol' SC.

Now you jest take fer instance,
Abert Rim, thet towers way up there,
An' kinda acts the part of guardian angel,
Fer them thet lives right near.

An' there's the valley spread below,
With wavin' fields of hay an' grass.
There's the hayin' season comin'
With the smell of new mown fields.
An' the satisfaction of yer knowin'
Thet the cold won't catch ya' wantin'
When it's snowin' an' it's blowin',
An' ragin' through the valley,
Lad or lass.

Heaven's found right here on earth,
Thet's a fact, now, so they say.
An' so, if thet be true,
An' things all point thet way,
I'm thinkin' thet new hand will tie a horse,
To the rail on the ol' front porch,
An' plan to git right down an' stay.

Oh yes, it's in the air,
An' rumor's floatin' wild an' free,
Thet there's a new cowhand
About to come on board
Out at the ol' SC.

We don't know jest yet,
As has been said right here before,
Jest who that rascal 's gonna be.

But one things sure as shootin,'
We're gonna love yer hand,
An' foot, an' toe,
an' every strand
Of hair ya grow,
No matter who ya might turn out 't be.

Myself, I've been a thinkin',
An' thet's mighty hard on me,
Of thet new babe who's comin' round
To take a hand,
An' make a brand
An' join the crew out there, ya see.
Yes sir! We're happy as can be,
'Bout the new cowhand a comin'
To the Lazy SC.

Doug Matheson

Struggles With the Why
Behind Difficult Questions

The limitations of my Hindi and my friends' English have not limited the things we have *tried* to discuss. Gathered around a few cheap plastic tables outside a café on a street in Salalah in southern Oman, the follow-on conversations after a shared meal of delicious curry and roti are sometimes trivial, but sometimes probing, deep, and honest. Our combined linguistic shortcomings have contributed to moments that run the gamut from hilarious, to frustrating, to awkward.

It has helped that when I do frequently need to resort to some English vocab, in this setting I reflexively do so in a south-Asian accent, which helps their understanding. If you've participated in or just listened to a conversation in which single sentences were a seemingly random conglomeration of Spanish and English, you can imagine our conversations. This circle of some of my local Pakistani and Indian friends has provided me with various elements of food for thought, and contributed very preliminary answers to a casual bet I made with some American friends.

In conversations with my local Omani friends, I don't have the Arabic ability to meet them half way as I do with the Hindi I learned in childhood, so I'm limited to conversation with fairly English-fluent friends, several of which I've made of adult students in my more advanced English classes.

In both of these conversational cases, I've sometimes pushed the envelope of what some would consider wise when you're the visitor in another country and culture. I've found though that many will engage in honest conversation when it's obvious you're not lecturing and you're not trying to assert sociocentric pride in your "superior" country or culture, even if some of the questions you're posing aren't easy, and may be thought-provoking to the point of troubling.

One of my Omani students directly asked me, "Why do you discuss difficult things with some of us? And why do you give us honest answers when you know that answer will trouble us?"

Why indeed would I be nutty enough to explore topics including science, politics, and religion, when those topics can make for rough sailing even when there are no linguistic or cultural hurdles to navigate?

I grew up a missionary kid in India, and was educated in Christian schools until graduate school. Despite a loving Christian indoctrination, I came to realize that when beliefs and evidence are in contradiction, personal honesty requires imposing the evidence on one's beliefs, and not the reverse. This path toward change and openness to new understanding was furthered by thought provoking experiences while teaching in Lebanon in 1980–81, and doing public health work in Rwanda from 1991 to April of 1994 and the beginnings of the genocide.

As a young man in my mid-twenties, I was confident that my God and my book were the "right" ones. When the fighting in Beirut flared, I asked my Lebanese students about who was fighting whom. It became clear that the notion of the crusades—we will fight for, die for, and kill for, our "right" Gods—is beyond dusty history books, it is alive and well, and still leads to people bleeding out, from bullets and bombs, if not swords and spears. This confidence in our various right gods has a dark side with a long track record.

As I slowly re-evaluated *my truths*, I tried to tell myself that the years it was taking were because of intellectual patience, and not because of my desire to find ways to end up keeping them. I knew that the Scientific Revolution was fueled in part by the realization that it was not only *okay* to question everything, including what had been viewed as authority and tradition, it was *good* to question... and then to test our ideas with the best honest (controlled) experiments we could design. And finally, and perhaps most importantly, to then be willing to accept verifiable evidence, even when we don't like what it points to, and thus be willing to recognize when we are wrong, and then to change our minds.

When exposed to Soren Kierkegaard's observation that "There are two ways to be fooled. One is to believe what isn't true. The other is to refuse to accept what is true," I simply added the conscious question: What have the centuries shown to be our best tool for slowly but surely figuring out what *IS* true? It seemed obvious that it has not been the conflicting claims based in different books, proclaiming different gods. And it seemed equally obvious that it has been the application of the approach of science—putting our ideas to objective tests, and then respecting the evidence, and changing, updating, our always-temporary conclusions.

It seemed clear to me that the value of a science-like approach should also apply to and would offer benefits in the social sciences—from history, to economics, to sociology, to anthropology, and... something else. If I went there, I knew I'd be stepping in it.

After I'd shed my religious filter for life's information and decision-making processes, I spent about a decade and a half just keeping that to myself. For nearly all the people I knew well, this wasn't a welcome conversation.

I had a new filter, what some would call a new bias. The track record of the approach of science, now with a half-millennium of history behind it, told me that this was the best and most honest way to evaluate and re-evaluate information and to make decisions on where I would stand on issues. But I didn't say anything to anyone about my internal change.

Many months after 9–11, as I watched our national focus shift away from al Qaeda and trying to capture Bin Laden, to the run-up to invading Iraq, I could read and hear which portion of America was urging caution and questioning

the justifications used, and which portion of America was gung ho about getting on with this invasion. The strong confidence I had witnessed (and I had had) as a young man, that "My God" was the *right* god, and by extension that "Our Book" and "Our People" were also *right*, easily led to people rallying to war "For God and Country."

It was then that I realized that anything resembling fundamentalist religion was not only *not* the solution, it was core to our problems, our tendency to draw sharp lines of Us vs. Them, and then being willing to quickly and enthusiastically turn those lines into action.

I had seen localized levels of chaos in Beirut, and then seen more ugly and much broader chaos in the launch into the genocide in Rwanda in April 1994, and so began to re-evaluate my silence.

In the sights and sounds and smell of death, I had seen the fabric of civilization significantly fray. I began to engage in conversation, to write, and to speak. I couldn't find a way to feel that I was being a responsible citizen of America or in a global sense, or being a responsible dad to my kids, if I kept silent about the risks that tend to go with strong faith.

In addition to the risk that those of strong faith tend to be quick to jump on the bandwagon of war in the name of their god, I shared two additional risks. The second is that those of strong faith tend to believe everything is in their god's hands, that there is a supernatural solution coming, and therefore that we don't need to take natural or man-made problems seriously, much less urgently. The third is that those of strong faith tend to have formed the habit of believing what they want to believe, and expecting those beliefs to be respected, which they interpret as going unchallenged.

When a person has repeatedly experienced an absence of direct challenge to his or her particular articles of faith, it does become a fairly absolute expectation, and—here's where it becomes very practical and problematic—it spreads from expecting religious beliefs to go unchallenged to expecting any number of personal beliefs to be respected, to be treated as equal alternatives, and to not be challenged.

I know a number of people of faith who manage to minimize to essentially zero the first two risks: more quickly jumping on the bandwagon of war in the name of their god, and dismissing problems because "It's all in god's hands and there's a supernatural solution coming." But the third risk—that we habituate to believing what we want and expect personal beliefs of nearly every type to go unchallenged—is much more insidious, much harder to successfully self-monitor against.

Although I've lived and worked in a number of places, I've lived and worked in rural Oregon for a few decades now, and I've watched America's recent drift toward increasing polarization. This is certainly multifactorial, but on all sides we must recognize it is not constructive. To work toward reducing this means increasing real communication, and reducing our temptation toward several things: living in well insulated, ideological echo chambers; equating opinions with facts; and expecting our beliefs to go unchallenged.

Some strenuously object to attempting to change the last point. They *want* to be able to believe any X, and to have that respected, to go unchallenged. Some have said, "So what if somebody believes in a flat earth, or young earth, or old earth, or intelligent design, or evolution? What difference does it make?"

That is an important question. I've been working on offering an answer to it both in America and in Oman.

Today most countries have some degree of democracy. We citizens are "passengers on the ship." We get to vote, and thus hire the crew which runs it. We can hire wise crews which consider the best of evidence in making decisions on

how to avoid the worst of troubled waters and dangerous shoals, or we can hire crews with firm and immune-to-change opinions because they are immune-to-the-evidence if they don't happen to already like it. This habituation to expecting our prior beliefs to be respected, to go unchallenged, shows up in very practical, concrete, ways.

Dismissing climate change has strong and direct parallels to dismissing the risks of tobacco (credit here to *Merchants of Doubt* by Naomi Oreskes), and this dismissal must be challenged. Dismissing the current risks to our national and global environment, air, land, and sea, must be challenged. Dismissing the risks of unnecessary and easily exacerbated cultural conflicts must be challenged. We can, and must, learn to move past the fairly human obsession with competing with "others." On a crowded planet with stressed ecosystems, meeting the sheer scale of the challenges of our times is going to require figuring out how to cooperate.

I feel I should clarify here what I've clarified many times, in many places: I'm not advocating that everyone should just become straight-up atheists. I *am* advocating that people of any and all faiths should moderate their faiths (recognizing that they could have been born into a culture and faith they now consider to be their worst enemy), and should consciously and actively self-monitor against these three risks so as to prevent the risks becoming realities. We can do better at the honest problem-solving and cooperation needed to meet the scale of today's problems.

Both in America and around those plastic tables outside my regular café in Salalah, I have asked a few extended questions. The first is, "What is the greatest determinant of most people's faiths?"

After some conversation, which sometimes meanders, but other times cuts right to the chase, we reach a consensus that it is the coincidence of birth...the family, culture, and century into which a person is born. We've illustrated this truth in *time* with Thor, Zeus, etc., and in *culture* with India-Pakistan, Iran-Saudi Arabia-Israel, Thailand, Mexico, and more. It isn't comfortable, but people get it.

The second question involves a more extended illustration.

I've asked my discussion partners to imagine a big hotel to which we bring two people of every faith on earth, including the many offshoots of all those faiths. From each faith, one of the two people must be a top priest, rabbi, scholar, mullah—highly educated in his faith's literature and dogma; the second person need not be a scholar, but should have a reasonable general education and be a very sincere believer.

These hundreds of people of faith, arranged in their pairs, are told that they will be provided with a comprehensive library, internet access, and food and water, and asked to create an initial document listing fifty central, important, beliefs of their faith, while including distinguishing beliefs which make their faith different. "You will all be locked in the hotel until you have met and discussed enough to persuade each other on what 'truth' is so that you can write out an agreement on *one* list of fifty truths, which 95% of you agree to."

"When will they come out of the hotel?" I ask.

My discussion partners always smile and say, "Never."

I then ask them to imagine a second hotel, to which we bring scientists who have various disagreements on broad or specific ideas held within science today.

These scientists make their lists of fifty things they hold to be true, again including some that are distinguishing (on which they disagree with others). Again, they are provided with food and water, a library and internet, *and* laboratory equipment and space as needed. They are then locked into this continuous science conference of a hotel where they

142

can meet, argue, go back to their labs for weeks, months, or years, and meet some more. They are told they can come out when their current lists have changed to where 95% of them agree on *one* list.

Again, I've asked when they'll come out. Each time my discussion buddies have been insightful enough to note that, while they might be stuck there for years, even for decades, they wouldn't be stuck there forever. They seem to know that while science isn't perfect, and there are strong egos and disagreements, science produces a forward movement as it develops consensus around ideas which are very well supported by verifiable evidence.

In both America and in Oman, the group response to these two questions and illustrations is neither completely uniform nor always good humored. I've seen people sit in stone-faced silence as others participated in lively discussion.

Now, you may remember a casual bet I mentioned at the outset of this conversation. As I contemplated my options on ending a career as a science and then history teacher, I looked around at America's increasing divides. I'd heard various Americans dismiss Muslims as close-minded and dangerous as a whole group, while considering themselves to be enlightened and open-minded.

It occurred to me that I could teach English in the Middle East, and live among and work with these Muslims. My casual bet was that I would find close-minded Muslims, *but* that I would also find open-minded ones, and that it wouldn't be starkly different than in our good ol' U.S. of A.

I've seen individuals doing open and honest exploration, with puzzled reevaluation-in-process written clearly on faces in both America and Oman. *And* I've seen that stone-faced silent resentment of any challenge to one's beliefs, and a clear unwillingness to even contemplate change in both our culture and theirs.

Some would suggest that I didn't choose to go try this

informal study surrounded by ISIS, and indeed I didn't. But I would point out that I'm not comparing this to the Westboro Baptist Church, either. Further, and more importantly, fundamentalist evangelical Christianity makes up a *much, much*, greater fraction of America's society than ISIS does within Islam.

Can we learn that (to quote Sen. DPM) "We're all entitled to our own opinions, but we're not entitled to our own facts"? Can we face the fact that some claims about reality (some beliefs) are indeed checkably connected to reality, and some *are not*? This fact is central to what makes opinions *not* all equal.

Among those in both cultures whose first reaction is resentful silence, some have hung around and ended up expressing themselves. And after I've listened to them, some of them have done a little more listening. I've shared that I realize I'm stepping on toes and it's often not welcome. But if the Titanic is headed for an iceberg and many passengers are preoccupied with sipping their tea and enjoying the beautiful sounds of a string quartet, efforts toward alerting more of the passengers and then hiring a crew, which pays deliberate attention to verifiable facts, it might turn out a lot better than not disturbing the peace until it is too late to make a difference.

In our recently more polarized American culture, some Facebook friends have posted fact-checkably wrong info. When I've challenged the point of their post, they've asked me to quietly move on if I don't like something they post. I've responded by encouraging them to challenge me if and when they feel I'm factually wrong, or on the wrong side of history. It has made little difference. It's as if too many now actually *prefer* their self- and technology-made echo-chamber. In order to be left alone in theirs, they offer the bargaining chip of leaving me alone in mine.

This is the something else I referred to as "stepping

144

in." Politics is ostensibly forbidden territory around the Thanksgiving table, but it has also become off limits if what you're about to do is break into a person's or a group's echo-chamber with other information or perspective.

If we're going to avoid the troubled waters and dangerous shoals our ship—or the whole ship of civilization—could face, we *need* informed, concerned, involved, and aware fellow-passengers who can and will engage in constructive conversations based in real, verifiable, facts. These conversations can't be expected to be easy or comfortable, but they can be civilized, and connected to checkable evidence in science and real lessons from history.

Here we are. I know people who genuinely think that other people of faith X or Y are thoroughly evil and must be fought, or are simply badly deluded and must not be accepted or allowed freedom, *while* they think their unique beliefs are right and make them part of this God's special people. They won't engage in an attempt at public dialogue on how we establish truth, won't thoughtfully challenge (very different than dismissing) other belief systems, because they don't want their own challenged. But they'll support a general cultural war *and* a military one aimed primarily at those "other" people.

I am sure that we *can* do better, and that we *must* do better. I continue to explore, to push frontiers, to ask uncomfortable questions—to see what we're willing to consider, to learn, and to check for ways in which we're willing to change.

Klamath Basin Writers

Crystal Moreno

WORTH IT

This sucks, she thought, shifting her weight from one leg to the other. Her feet wouldn't stop hurting and it was making her angry and unfriendly. No one else in line would talk to her, put off by the bitchiness of her expression. She was okay with that. She watched the others who had reached the front of the line take their boxes, brimming with gaily wrapped toys, walk off with their families and climb into warm, waiting cars and speed off to a nominally happy holiday.

She tried to correct herself, her thinking. She didn't know if those who were surrounded by what seemed to be happy relatives were really luckier, were really happier. They just looked like it, didn't mean that home was happy and not just poor.

That's what the Salvation Army Christmas handout line meant anywhere, really, but in a small rural white community especially.

It meant that you were bottom-of-the-barrel-fucked and that those grateful faces were just spur of the moment happy. It meant that she had no right to judge the faces of her brethren. She shifted her feet again, because *goddamn, they hurt*, and hoped she'd be able to get through the line fast enough to get to walk to work on time.

She shuffled forward three steps and tried to walk like nothing was wrong. She felt as though she succeeded. She realized she was jealous. Everyone else had a ride, at least the women.

There were men in line. You could tell they were just there for the food box, maybe the blankets. They would sell the toys later. She was the only woman on foot.

She was the only black woman.

She stood out like a sore thumb and she hated her own vulnerability. She was obviously so many layers of disadvantaged. Poor, minority, friendless. A walking target.

Good looking and young with it, too. More
disadvantage, that had encouraged a few in line to come
at. Predators were always around. She was getting better at
spotting them.

The man behind her, standing so close she could feel
his breath ruffle the curls on her neck and the brush of his
jean jacket when he swayed. He stank, not just unwashed
clothes but unwashed body, like he'd given up, like he didn't
care. She cared. Her little family was always clean.

She was pulled away from internal reverie.

Another predator approached. An older, white woman,
who looked friendly at first, until the woman got close and
the sad lines in her face and the caged look in her eyes spoke
volumes about a broken heart and a broken life.

She'd felt for that soul, had almost let her cut in
line because she saw the slick lookin' Mexican dude in
the parking lot. The one with the to fancy paint job of a
big-breasted chick straddling an Aztec chief on the hood of
his ride.

She wondered about the woman's kids, wondered
what white lady had traded of her children's innocence for
that guy to afford said auto detail on the hood of his whip and
felt her heart get cold.

No.

Her own feet were wet because she walked three
miles in the dirty slush of snow, in old tennis shoes that
didn't quite fit anymore, to stand in line to get her kid a
charity gift. Felt her anger rise and prod at her. She worked,
hard. Two jobs—and still couldn't afford Christmas miracles
for her kid. She'd be goddamned if her baby didn't get a little
wonderful out of the world because this poor white woman
didn't have the ability to stand up to some narcissistic dick.

So she'd given the woman a hard-eyed glare, seen the
false eagerness bleed out of the woman's expression, replaced
by something uglier and true as white lady stalked to the
back of the line.

Damn, now her feet hurt worse and she was bothered

with the necessity to watch her six. She shuffled forward again. She began to rock, wondering idly if cold feet were supposed to feel like they were on fire, trying to recall hypothermia facts, before dismissing the line of thought as melodramatic.

She hoped she looked bored and not in pain. Bored was safer.

The line continued, and when she finally reached the front desk—a small folding table with a rusted metal chair and an extremely fat man sitting on it, she gave her social security number. He gauged her, starting at her feet and working his way up, lingering on her breasts.

He looked disappointed, and she felt a petty moment of satisfaction until he lumbered himself off of his seat, and tottered toward the cardboard box she knew had been marked for her, and removed an item.

She tried not to show her disappointment when he returned, as she gazed down into the box. A block of butter, three boxes of mac and cheese, a can of chili, a can of green beans and one Purple dinosaur toy. Not wrapped.

She signed her name on a piece of paper and thanked him politely. Picked the box up in her hands and walked by the long line of others. Some smirked, some looked at her with pity.

She wasn't certain which made her angrier.

She exited the building and felt the cold bite of winter wind hit the tip of her nose first and grab her tired feet second. She adjusted her grip on the box; the cans had slid to one side making it heavier on that end. She set it down on the sidewalk, took off her coat, and used it to cover the unwrapped toy.

She picked up the box again and smiled, trying not to cry. From the loss of dignity, self-pity, or physical pain, she wasn't' certain, but thinking of her child, thinking of Christmas, she hoped he would like the toy, and she set off.

The longer she walked, the more she thought of his happiness. After a while, her feet didn't hurt so much after all.

TRUMP

This short essay, told from very different perspectives, is an attempt at coherency that the American people have been expressing regarding the impact that personal experiences have had on their political views. While it may fall short in its efforts for a certain amount of levity, at its core it is my own attempt to point out the validity of concern that all voices possess, even when we neglect to filter out self-interest, rather than the greater good of the recognition of common humanity that unites us all...

Love and Potential Zealotry

Do I love President Trump? That might, perhaps be to strong a word. I do admire the man, and what so many left-wing, liberal nay-sayers fail to recognize is that the American people finally have someone in the white house that will 'tell it like is'. None of the ten- dollar words that generally dribble out of the mouths of most politicians.

Trump is a self-made man, a billionaire even, that embodies the ideals of what has traditionally made this nation the greatest on earth; hard work, plain talk and the rights of the common folk, all based on a solid foundation of Christian beliefs.

Trump might not be able to come right out and say it, but that man knows that abortion is a sin and the people's government shouldn't be funding it, the way they did when socialist Obama was in office. The other thing I really admire about Trump is that he's not afraid to stand up for white people.

Now I'm not racist when I say that, I have black friends and I know Mexican people, too. But as a white man in America, we get blamed for everything, black-on-black crime, rape culture, dirty cops, hell, even "white privilege."

"I grew up poor, my daddy was a dirt farmer and my momma was a drunk, I don't know what 'privilege' there is in that. I bettered myself through hard work and never asked for any hand-outs. I don't love Trump, but I do think he can make America great again, now if you'll excuse me, I have an NRA meeting to get to.

Hate and What We've Learned

I read somewhere once, that at the root of hate lies fear and that's how I know that for the first time in my life, I hate our American president. Even when I disagreed, or my chosen candidate lost, I never hated the winner. Even when I didn't like either candidate, I always cast my ballot for the one I thought would do the least amount of damage, even when I couldn't actively admire the individual.

Perhaps it was naïve on my part, but I never disparaged the victor because I believed, on an intrinsic level, that whoever won held the best interests of the American people to be a sacred trust. A little tarnished, a little dented but still, sacred.

I don't believe that anymore, not because of the cult of personality that Trump surrounds himself with, or the constant revisionist history that he uses to mask his failures and ignorance. It's not even Trump's titanium coated sense of entitlement, glossed with a sheen of privilege so thick it sparks a harsh glare on every camera lens.

I despise the president because I've started to fear the zealotry buried in the eyes of my neighbors, the lingering looks on the faces of people in my community that I've worked and lived alongside for the better portion of my life.

I hate Trump when an acquaintance and I casually pass the time and the presidents campaign slogans roll off

their tongue. I can never tell if the person is aware of the complex layers of hate buried in the phrase they just uttered or if they're mindlessly, happily spewing out jargon that shields them from independent thought, and I can't decide which state is worse.

I hate Trump because I'm afraid of the infection that he represents, an insidious thing whose symptoms were once lit with torches at nighttime and captured by black and white newsreels in Europe.

I think I should hate the man's ineptitude on the global level, his blatant heavy handedness when we live in a nuclear age, but we've lived in that world for so long that the thought of obliteration at enemy hands, is understood with a certain fatalism.

I despise him because the passage of wind that powerful individuals generally leave in their wake has never passed by me so close or so cold, and my hate is fear and humanity's past justifies it presence.

The Cynicism of Reality

People think that we no longer live in a society in which one can engage in passionate, respectful discourse involving opposing political or philosophical ideals.

Those people are correct, we don't live in that society. What people often fail to consider is that we've never lived in that society. No one has ever lived in that society and before anyone utters the words 'bloodless coup' let me counter that with the phrase 'internal politics.'

We are, for the most part, 'the masses' and the 'one percenters' aren't necessarily those with means to establish wealth but also power. This can mean the power of influence in an Oligarchy but that in America we term Constitutional Democracy. Tomato, tah-mah-to. Point being, that the majority of us simply aren't privy to the behind-the-scenes chaos that ensues when an unpopular American president attains office.

No matter one's thoughts or feelings on President Trump or the media ratings scramble that plays on the public's short memory, he is by no means the first polarizing figure in the oval office.

Liberals rail against the current administration, citing each action undertaken by the west wing as heralding the collapse of the American infrastructure and the enslavement of the population enmasse, while Conservatives rally staunchly around their chosen candidate as a champion defender to preserve the American way of life and save us all from godless communism.

This has happened before, simply with each party's rhetoric shifting, dependent on whose candidate has supremacy. While no one can deny the tidal impact of a presidents influence on the thoughts and minds of the people, and whether one sees that as a positive or a negative, a (cold) measure of comfort can be taken from the fact any president is a bit of a figurehead with clearly marked limitations on executive powers, like the three laws of robotics but hopefully with a better outcome.

CONTEMPLATION

"He was the love of my life. He was a good man." My mother is in my garden, sitting in the gazebo and chatting on her phone with another of the myriad relatives I don't speak with anymore, haven't in years. I stir a little creamer in my coffee as I stand in my kitchen and eavesdrop through the window. It's early, not yet six, and I let the sound of birdsong drown out the rest of her conversation, as I get lost in my own thoughts on the subject of her statement.

She's talking about my late stepfather, and it takes me a moment to recall exactly how long he's been dead. I mentally crunch a few numbers and realize with a mild start that it's been twenty-three years. She's mentioned him a lot during this visit, trying to get me to traipse down memory lane with her, but her interpretation of that path is rosier than my own. I think that's the reason the man remains a contentious topic of conversation between us, and her statement is only partially correct.

He might've been the love of her life but he wasn't really a good man, though he wasn't necessarily an evil one either; he was simply a weak one. I finally take a sip of my coffee and make a moue of distaste—too much cream. I dump it out and get a fresh cup, taking this one black. I savor the first sip of the strong Sumatran brew and continue to ponder.

My mother is a highly manipulative narcissist. An ex-junkie with hoarding issues, and he was an ex-preacher turned alcoholic who thought he could knock around my fourteen-year-old self until I put him in his place and broke his arm. I suppose they *had* been perfect for each other.

My mother breezes through the back door, pulling

me from my internal musings and gives me a sunny smile, accompanied with a cheerful "Good morning!"

I smile back and return the greeting, internally bracing myself for our dysfunctional dance of "pretend." Pretending we like each other (we don't) and trying not to forget that we love each other (we do).

We spend the rest of her two-week visit in carefully enforced amicability, avoiding any conversational topics of dissension, like walking through a shit covered field to reach the other side with moderately clean boots. She refers to her late husband as "Your dad" a mere 3,200 more times, and I gently and adamantly correct her 3,200 more times with, "He wasn't my dad."

When she finally returns to her home state, waving from the train window to where I stand on the platform, I'm so giddy with being relieved of her presence that if I were an old-time cowboy with a set of six shooters, I would fire them repeatedly into the air and do a Yosemite Sam style dance.

As the next few days go by though, I find myself becoming more contemplative, unable to dismiss thoughts of my late stepfather from my own mind. I believe very few peoples' lives can be seen as wholly evil or entirely good. No matter how society tries to categorize individuals as monsters or saints, the ironic dichotomy is that we're both and neither, for the most part.

My stepfather embodied that also, no matter the wary respect we displayed toward each other during his life. After his arm healed, he never raised a hand against me again. We were never nice to each other, but as an adult, looking back over the turbulent years of my adolescence—how I was already fourteen years old when we first met—I can recall times when he genuinely tried for a human connection with me that my stony heart always rebuffed. I think of how my

mother's affection for us both was a frail bridge neither he or I could meet in the middle of.

I'm glad she loved someone like that though, in a "love of my life," kind of way. I can never say it, get the words out right, because the conversation always devolves into my frustration with her expectation that I feel that way too. That talk ends with her genuine affront, the emotionally manipulative display of her hurt because I can't (won't) relive memories I was never a part of, as though my mother and I aren't entirely separate entities.

I think of how when my phone rings and I see it's my mom, I only answer it every one-out-of-three times because I can't put it all into words that she'll understand or listen to.

I think on all this a week or so after my mother has returned to her home state, and I'm standing in my kitchen again, on another quiet morning with my cup of coffee going cool on the countertop. I wonder all of these things with my cell phone held to my ear, listening to the sound of ringing, echoing softly over the line, waiting for my own daughter to pick up.

KLAMATH BASIN WRITERS

Jim Olson

THE CRATER

It was November 1944, northern Europe, in the middle of WWII. First squad of Charlie Company was on a recon mission. It was cold and cloudy with a slight breeze giving the air a painful bite.

Joe Bradley was corporal, which made him second in command of the patrol. Joe came from Bend, Oregon, and lied about his age when he enlisted.

Joe soon discovered his mistake. Nothing was what he thought it would be. He found heroism only existed in newspapers and books. On patrols like this, fear was what consumed everyone. No one had any control of whether he lived or died. Those mortars and large bombs fell out of the sky randomly, not looking for anyone in particular. If a guy were in the wrong place at the wrong time, his number was up. It had become that simple.

"Spread out!" commanded the sergeant. Everyone silently obeyed.

They only went about fifty yards when the mortars started coming in again. Swishshshsh. The men could hear them coming through the air, so they took cover as always. The mortars were falling close by. Joe could feel the ground shake with each explosion. One came very close and he cupped his hands over his ears and closed his eyes as tight as possible.

When the air was silent again, the sergeant yelled, "Move out. Let's go!"

The men were creeping through the trees when a shot rang out and everyone hit the dirt again. Joe looked around trying to see where the sniper was. He looked at the man to his left and could see he had been hit. One of the men took a shot into the shrubs up ahead and soon everyone was

firing in the same direction. Joe got the shakes immediately and soon the mortars were coming in again, along with some heavier stuff. Another round hit very close and Joe panicked. He jumped to his feet and started running. He was in such a panic he left his rifle laying on the ground. He was running toward the enemy out of sheer fear when a shell exploded right in front of him, lifting him in the air.

When Joe woke up there was gunfire all around him. The pain in his leg was unbearable. He could feel blood running down his cheek. He put his hand up to feel how bad it was. He had been slightly grazed, but it was bleeding bad enough that he thought he should get out his little first-aid kit and put a bandage on it.

That's when he noticed a dead German soldier in the same crater. He also noticed more wounds on his legs. Seeing this it made the pain seem much worse. His right boot was opened up and smoke was coming out. He could smell the smoke and burning flesh. Joe couldn't bear to look at it any longer.

It had gotten quieter now that the patrol had moved on ahead. *God, I hope those guys come and find me soon.* He worried about his legs, especially the right one. Joe knew another group would be moving up to get the wounded and dead. He hoped it would be soon.

As Joe was trying to get comfortable he noticed a movement from the other soldier. He immediately started looking for his rifle, then remembered he'd left it behind. *How stupid can you get! I'm a dead son of a bitch now.* He grabbed his trench knife from his ammo belt and held it up. The soldier could see it glistening in the light. It was large and sharp enough to shave with.

The soldier moaned in pain and started looking around. He spotted Joe lying there. "You gonna stick me with that?"

"Maybe. If you try for that gun of yours," Joe answered.

"I'm out of ammo. We've been cut off from the supply line."

"How come you speak good English?"

"I grew up in Redding, California."

"What the hell are you doing in that uniform?"

"'Bout ten years ago my father took us back to the father land," he claimed, shaking his head as if he knew it was the wrong move.

"So, you became a soldier?"

"In Germany you have three choices—join the military, go to prison, or get shot for desertion!"

"Holy shit!" Joe replied in disbelief. "Is that for real?"

They lay there sizing each other up. Joe slowly put his knife away. It didn't look as if he would need it, at least not right now. He noticed the soldier was bleeding badly from his arm and also had a leg wound. He looked in his first aid kit and found another bandage but wasn't sure if it was large enough.

"Where you from?" the soldier asked.

"Near Bend, Oregon."

"Oh yeah! We went fishing there...bout a year before we left."

"Do you realize how ridiculous this is. We lived about, what, three hundred miles from each other and here we are in this stinking crater."

"I know. I didn't want to go to war but, like I said, wasn't much choice."

"I guess someone else don't like the war either. They tried to kill that crazy bastard Hitler a while back."

"I wish they had succeeded. He is destroying Germany."

Then they heard the mortars sizzling through the air again and they both put their heads down and covered up the best they could.

The mortars kept coming for what seemed like a long

162

time. They exploded all around them, some were close and some farther away. When the shelling stopped, both men relaxed and lay there staring at the clouds rolling by. The air was thick with the smell of cordite and dust. Nearly enough to choke on.

"Well, it sounds like your supply lines are open again. My name is Joe. What's yours?"

"Ben," the German answered, almost laughing.

"Sompin' funny 'bout that?"

"Who could have dreamed such a thing? The two of us in this hole like this," Ben answered almost silently. "In case you haven't noticed, we are in deep shit."

"Well, one of us is, we just don't know which one yet," he replied wincing in pain. "If my guys come first I won't let them hurt ya, but they'll take you prisoner."

"If they don't get here soon they won't have to worry about it."

"I've got some bandage left over. If you can trust me to get close enough to put it on."

"We can't do much to each other anyway. Let's call a truce. I think the war is probably over for us anyway," Ben said holding his arm in pain.

Joe started to move toward him but the pain in his legs changed his mind. He lay there trying to wish the pain away.

"I might be able to scoot over there," Ben said as he started dragging himself toward Joe.

Joe could see that Ben was in a lot of pain, also. He got next to Joe but was exhausted and just lay back and took some deep breaths. Joe got his trench knife out and Ben reacted in fear.

"Just gonna cut your sleeve! I swear I won't break our truce!"

"I guess I don't have much choice. Do I?" Ben said wincing in pain.

Joe cut Ben's sleeve and saw a nasty wound that was opened up to the bone. "Look, you're going to need stitches, I think. Yeah, I'm not a medic but..."

"Just do what you can. I don't want to bleed to death."

"I can put a tourniquet on it, but you will have to loosen it every so often. You know, to let the blood get to your arm."

"Whatever!"

When Joe finished he laid back, not believing how much it had wore him out. "If I go to sleep be sure to loosen that every ten or fifteen minutes. You don't want to lose that arm."

They lay there resting for quite a while when Ben said, "I always planned on going back to California. I kind of doubt if they will ever let me go back now."

"This world is so screwed up, who knows what'll happen," Joe said as he looked over at Ben. Then they lay quietly for a while.

"Ben, what day is today?"

"I don't know. Doomsday, I think."

"You know what I mean!"

Then the mortars started coming again. They were exploding all over the place. It seemed to be a lot more than earlier and lasted a lot longer. Both men lay there covering up the best they could, their bodies jerking with each explosion.

Finally, Joe started yelling to the top of his lungs. "Stop it, dammit. Stop it you crazy bastards!" And just as suddenly as it started, it stopped.

"Well that's one way to stop it," Ben said as he looked up.

"I'm sorry. I didn't mean to yell like that. It just came out of my mouth. They're sure using a lot of mortars. Who do they think they have here, a general?"

Again, it got quiet for several minutes.

"Friday, I think," Ben stated out of the blue.

"WHAT?!"

"Friday. You asked me what day it was. Not sure, but I think it's Friday."

"Oh yeah. Friday. All my friends are having a malted at the soda shop and here I am in this stinking hole. I just can't stand to think I'm here and they're home having a good time." Joe reached into his pocket and pulled out a small pack of smokes. He started looking for a match to light it. "Shit! I can't even have a smoke."

"Well, I have a lighter and you have some smokes. I think we can work it out."

Joe handed him a smoke and Ben lit them both. "I can tell you what. American cigarettes are a hundred times better than...hell, they're better than anywhere."

They lay there trying to enjoy their smokes.

"When I signed up I was wanting to fight the Japs. You know, because of Pearl Harbor. I had no desire to come to Europe," Joe explained. Then after a minute he said, "I wonder what Julie is doing right now."

"Is she your girl?"

"Well she was until I told her I was joining up. She got pissed and said if I joined we were through," Joe answered, shaking his head as if he didn't believe it. "I hope she will forgive me when I get home."

"Tell me about her...everything."

"Nah, be a waste of time," Joe claimed as he blew the last of his smoke into the air.

"Too bad. Nuthin' else to do," Ben said holding his arm and wincing in pain. He then loosened the tourniquet. "Oh, dam that hurts! Holy shit!"

It got quiet again as Ben tried to regain his composure.

"She is about five foot six, light brown hair. Oh, that smile, you wouldn't believe it. Greatest smile you ever seen. She has just a few freckles across her nose." Joe started laughing. "She was always covering them up with make-up. I told her I liked them, made her look very special."

"Keep going. I am beginning to see her."

"Oh, man, she had such lips. I haven't kissed many girls but I would bet she is the best kisser ever." Another long pause. "I love to hear her laugh. I really miss her. I hope she at least thinks about me once in a while."

"I'd bet she misses you, too."

"You got a girl back home?"

"Not really. I had my eyes on a real beauty but she didn't even see me. Everybody liked her. She had her choice of any guy she wanted. Why the hell would she see me? I dreamt about her every night for a long time. Painful, real painful." Then both guys laughed. "I thought about finding another girl, you know, one who liked me, but I couldn't get her out of my mind. I think she destroyed me without so much as a glance."

"How do they get so much control over us?"

"Hell if I know."

It got quiet again and Joe started feeling the pain in his lower right leg. Sweat was pouring off Joe's face. "Damn, I wish we could help somehow," Ben said.

"I have a little tube of morphine but I'm afraid I might need it worse later, so I'm saving it. How much sense does that make? I wonder why the pain comes and goes like that."

"Well, at least it goes for a while."

"Ben, I hope when this is over you can come back to the States. I would like to hook up with you then."

"Yeah, well we'll see. Hey, did you hear that? Sounded like twigs breaking."

Joe tried to look over the top of the crater. "I can't get up there enough to see."

Ben tried to scoot up higher. "I don't see anything yet." He kept looking around but didn't see anyone out there.

Then Ben slid back down. "Hell, I don't care who finds us, your guys or mine. We need some medical help!"

"Hey, there it is again," Joe said, trying to stretch and see over the top again. "Did you hear that?"

"I sure did!" Ben scooted back up to the top. The noise was getting louder and closer. Someone was breaking branches as they walked through.

"Do you see them yet? Is it my guys or yours?"

Ben slid back down with a look of terror on his face. He was white as a ghost.

"Well, who is it?"

"A BEAR!"

KLAMATH BASIN WRITERS

Alex Spenser

On Being Peace - A Meditation

In the quiet, I dream of clarity - and so it begins. There is a moment of emotion and light where wonder, beauty, and love come together in the essence of understanding. That is the moment I call peace.

We stand again on a precipice. When we stand here in this place, it is rare to look back, because fear has us looking at the fall before us, the fall we must take to continue.

For a moment, with the wind encircling us, let us take in the silence, hear the hum of the world around us, and feel our feet. The ground beneath them is solid and sure. It is our perception that we fear, and feeling the earth beneath us, we have the strength to turn with the breeze and look back upon where we have been: the triumphs of the year, and the sorrows; the beauty and the anger; the wonder of new lives born to us, and the tragedy of those lost.

And-we-breathe.

All of it becoming a part of who we are and who we will ever be.

And-we-breathe.

Relaxing into our new reality.

And-we-breathe.

Relaxing into our love and beauty and wonder and we - in this moment - accept. We accept who we are now, and who we have ever been. We accept who we will become and - in this moment - we turn again, and instead of the ground far below us, we realize the breeze. We feel the wind and know it is a part of us as well as the sky, and we find our wings, feel them resting against our backs, where they have ever been, and we step from the purity of the earth into the vast assurance of the sky...

And we fly!

Realizing we are fledglings, in the first moments, we do flutter as we find the current, we do dip into the pockets of what feels like nothing. And then, as if the gods are holding us upon fingertips of gold, and starlight - we soar and embrace this new moment, and we fly! Touching the clouds of dreams, the clouds that are the people we love and know as our surety in the world, and the clouds who are those friends we have yet to meet. People we have yet to love and dream with.

We look to see the brilliant sunshine and realize the warmth of the sun is peace, the peace that will heal us. The peace that will heal the world - and we touch it, hold it, let it surround us. It becomes us and as we see the earth, and know it is time to land into the reality of this moment.

The peace has given us a new light, a new aura of being. And, with the instinct that is innate in beings that fly, we see our place on the earth, slow the wind with our wings, and with a gentle hover above our place in the world, we step out of flight with the knowledge that we need only feel the breeze flutter our feathers to take flight again, and renew our connection to the peace that is ours - the peace that lives in the rays of the sun, the peace that gives us the strength to be and love and create this world beautiful.

ON THE BUILDING BLOCKS OF A LIFE

The goal is to see a world of acceptance, a place where people are free to be whomever they are. The danger of the world stems from those who are afraid. Everyone is love. Everyone is a child in need of love and acceptance, and when children are loved and accepted, they become adults who know how to love and accept.

We are, each of us, every age we ever were. Once we have accomplished being a five year old, we add on being six. We are a cumulation of our experiences.

Every year has the responsibility of holding up every year before it, the twenty year old, must care for the two year old within.

We are everyone we ever were. We are the kid who got picked last and the one who ran the bases in the ninth inning to win the game. We are all of our accomplishments and all of our failings. We learn when we mis-step. We move forward and engage our brains and get through to the next moment. And, if there is a team of players who accept themselves, they are a team who will accept each other and acceptance is a motivating factor.

Each year builds upon the last, giving us an interesting, and unique foundation of time, and, if we hypothesize that all time is one, we are who we have ever been. The challenges we have faced head-on and those we have shied away from, the time we hit it out of the park, and the moment we were the reason the team lost the game.

We are programmed to learn more from adversity than beauty, because we need to remember adversity to save our lives. We are charged with nurturing all of our selves and creating a life where all children are cared for. If we see ourselves as eternal children, eternal humans, and we find

compassion for ourselves, we will have the ability to find compassion for others.

It is about people accepting themselves - who they ever were - and through the acceptance of themselves, accepting others.

Re-integrating all we ever were and accepting. Accepting the good and the failings we perceive in ourselves, and accepting the good as good, and the failings as acceptable nuances that have given us strength and wisdom. It is by failing, that we begin to succeed. We have to know falling down hurts to be motivated to walk.

Acceptance is Peace

All of humanity will find peace when they accept themselves and, through self-acceptance will find the strength to accept others.

ON INJUSTICE AND PEACE

When we witness injustice in the world we must speak out against it.

This begins with the small injustices: a word of malice said against a friend that we know to be untrue, a word against a man or woman because of their manhood or womanhood, a word against people for their beliefs, for their sexual orientation, for the color of their skin.

These injustices seem small in the locker room, at a party, in the office. When allowed to live - injustice becomes emboldened, strengthened by the turn of the cheek, the obligatory giggle. That person is emboldened by the ability to say these things without consequence; the person who listens is also emboldened to carry out the manner and message of injustice. If those words came and were accepted without consequence, that person is emboldened to believe that their words of injustice will also be accepted without consequence.

This is the time to remember that in America we are entitled to free speech; and this entitlement we hold dear, has its consequences.

Standing up for that kid in the hallway could mean a world at peace. Every action of peace raises the bar, is witnessed and engaged with, and creates, moment-by-moment, an atmosphere of peace, a place of kindness, an opportunity for love.

When we speak out against injustice, those who are witness to our strength are emboldened to speak out themselves against other injustices. We owe it to ourselves as humans to speak up, to stand up, one by one and say:

this person is worth being stood up for; this person and every person is worth our kindness, even when, and perhaps **especially** when we disagree with them.

The next time you hear someone speak with injustice about your friend, or about someone you work with, or someone you don't know at all - perhaps you will stand up for that person. Your strength will be witnessed, and you will embolden that person, who will embolden the next person who has the power to create peace.

An Action of Peace

We stand firm.

We believe in what is good for each person, each individual, her or his own goals and beliefs, and those are what we stand for.

We stand for the rights of everyone.

We stand for the ability of the shyest among us to speak her truth, the weakest among us to dream his dreams, the strongest among us to reach heights that most of us find difficult to imagine until we see that they have been reached by one amazing individual, and when the bar is raised we all rise to meet it.

We see possibility and it changes us, it moves us, motivates us to experience our own minds and bodies in different ways.

We are amazing in our capacities to grow and be and live in a world with ever-widening boundaries.

SOMETHING WONDERFUL IS HAPPENING!
SATURDAY OCTOBER 21, 2017

On the cover of my journal I have written "Something Wonderful is Happening!" and, therefore, it is. Words are magnets and these words I read every time I look at my journal give my brain the fodder it needs to begin creating the positive moments I want to live in.

The power of our minds to create our lives is amazing!

We, here in America, and reverberating across the planet, have endured more than our usual share of disaster from the mass shooting in Las Vegas, to the wildfires in California and Oregon, and the devastation in the wake of hurricanes and typhoons across the planet. We are all reeling from the destruction of lives and the pain and suffering of the aftermath.

Still people are homeless and without electricity and clean water by the tens of thousands in our own Puerto Rico, a month after hurricane Maria blasted the small island. Signs throughout Las Vegas remind us to be "Vegas Strong" and fires still burn as we find 220,000 acres decimated, 5,700 structures destroyed and at least forty people dead over more than half a dozen counties in Northern California.

And the front cover of my journal says: "Something Wonderful is Happening!"

When the fires began on October 8, I was at a beautiful hot springs in far eastern California, and, as the day pressed

on, more and more evacuees came to rest and breathe in the tranquility of the sanctuary. I had planned to be on the road in northern California that day, and the plans changed without reason and, as so often happens, the reason revealed itself in a very unsubtle way.

I was enjoying the solace of the hot springs and was a witness to two different views of the fires. One woman was acting as if she were there, being engulfed by the flames, all the while recounting her knowledge that her home, her things, and her family were safe. Another woman, while looking into the beautiful fire of the cast iron stove said: "...It's beautiful, and this is what my home looks like right now. This is beautiful, and one hundred percent contained..." with a slight smile in her voice.

The first woman was devastated in the beautiful place. The second was grateful to be so fortunate to be where she was. And both reactions to the situation were real, valid, and worthy of my respect.

They were both great teachers.

Our minds are creative and we can choose how we see the world. We can look at the things that happen around us and accept and allow the flow of energy to be as it will, or we can rage against the things we have no control over.

There are actions we can take to secure ourselves against future disaster: Common sense gun regulation and care for our environment can make a great difference for the future. And in this moment we must continue to breathe, continue to care for ourselves and those around us, and continue to love and give our brains the option of something Wonderful happening.

Klamath Basin Writers

The Masks We Live in: Peace, Love, and Standing in Your Truth
(Written on the Occasion of Halloween and a Blue Moon)

Creating our most wonderful selves, that is the goal of this grand journey we have embarked upon. Whether by choice or fate we find ourselves in this moment, together in this place with a reverence for community.

We move through each day, creating as we go, the person we want people to see. We tend to hide behind what we do or who we wish to be. The masks of our day-to-day being-ness are many. We don one for our friends, one for those people we pass on the street, and another for the police officer we pass on the highway, as we check the gauges and wonder if the mediation of driving has taken us away from the reality of driving, or has it awakened our senses in such a way that the meditation of the road itself is keeping us safe.

We have learned through a lifetime of fear and shame that we are to hide our true selves, that we are to disguise the humanity. We are taught to hold back tears when we are sad, hold back laughter when we are happy, and keep our dreams to ourselves.

We crave peace. We crave a journey that will enlighten. We crave moments that light us up.

Our childhood directives that have become the ruts in our life roads, leading us like slot cars to some final destination of banality, betray our cravings for our journey of peace and enlightenment. These ruts have been honed in fear and self- judgment that we inherited or just picked up along the way.

There is a choice to be made in every moment in

178

time. There is a choice to be ourselves, the one we wake up with every morning and know to be good and kind and open. The self we know with an intimacy that we share with a very precious few.

Every moment, every tick of the clock, every wave that encompasses the sand and sends the tiny crabs scampering. Every motion of the trees that betrays the presence of the breeze. Every stretch of the cat, every moment of a newborn's life... We make a choice to be authentic, or to don our mask once again.

We get to choose. We hold that freedom of choice as inherent in this wonderful place we live. The self-evident truths have become mired in the fear and pain of our daily lives. And, we have a choice, a choice in this moment to stand for ourselves in a journey of kindness, a journey of grace, a journey of truth.

Truth—the illusive being that lies within us—that we fear so much to express. We deserve our expression of truth, our expressions of the moments we hold dear. It is time to stand in our own truths, delve into our deepest selves, and discover who we are, who we were always meant to be.

Our moon is full tonight. It is blue and beautiful, unabashed in its willingness to move the tides once more before the last breath of October is exhaled. It is a beginning, a motion, a moment to embrace. Our tiny moon is there expressing itself, calling upon us to seize this moment in time that we might stand up and find our truth, to be in our three year old selves and say I Declare Peace.

I declare this with this planet, this moment is one of peace and I create this peace by standing in my truth. And now we take the baton our beautiful blue moon is handing us, and run, play, writhe with the emotion that is our inheritance, the truth of our being-ness, to allow our lives to flourish, to allow our lives to align with those around us, knowing that we share this space because we have something to share—our emotions, our thoughts, our breath of love, and devotion to one another.

Standing in Truth is the goal of this life. Crafting a lasting peace is the goal of this life. Moving the beings on this planet to recognize the love within each of us and release it out of ourselves into the cosmos, knowing that the more love we share, the more the font is filled, the more we express, the more the love is there to express.

Find joy. Find love. Live this moment in the truth of yourself. Cast away the masks of fear and Embrace love and Spread it out across this lovely, breathing planet of ours, and Declare Peace.

Cathy Williams

THE OLD HOUSE

She sat back in the faded lawn chair. Memories poured in. Births, deaths, wedding, funerals. Even, at one point, a standoff. She and her Old House had lived a long and mostly happy life.

"Not that we're done for yet," she told the veranda.

Visions of her new husband carrying her across the threshold. Their first kiss as husband and wife on that very step. Their first fight in the kitchen just around that corner. "How dare he tell me his mother could teach me to cook!" she chuckled.

The seven babies conceived and born in the big corner bedroom with the porch all its own.

The time she stood her ground and proudly went her way. The sadness of her beloved Spencer's departing.

She was happy her granddaughter wanted the house. Only she could love it as much as she, herself, had. As she watched the new bride carried over the threshold she felt a gentle hand on her elbow.

She turned to see Spencer. "It's time to leave this Old House, and come to a new one with me."

THE VASE

It looked like a great idea in that little shop
    Sitting on the shelf.
But now I get it home, I'm not sure it fits in.
    I guess I should take it back.
I'll put it on the bookcase for now.

Every time I dust, I'm gonna return it.
    It's too tall to fit on the bookshelf.
Set it on the desk.
    It's out of place there, too.
I keep moving it around, intending to take it back.

Then, one day winter is over,
    And spring wakes up my garden.
I cut a variety of stalks, stems, buds, and blossoms.
    I start an arrangement.

My out-of-place, too-tall Vase comes to life.
    I set it on that little table by the window,
The one where the sun comes in.
    I'm amazed at the transformation.
She has found her place.

And I realize
    We are all like that—
A great idea at first, then a shred of doubt,
    A feeling of being useless,
And of being out of place.

But once we fill ourselves with our traits and our talents,
    Once we find our Niche,
Then the transformation takes place.
    And we really are a Great Idea.

THE MAN ACROSS THE WAY

1.

The man across the way caught her attention right off—for no reason she could think of. Neither word, nor action denoted recognition. Maybe that was it. Surrounded by revelry, he sat alone, unmoving. Why should she be so enthralled? Was she, herself, not here to be quiet and left alone to garner some peace? She forced herself to look away, telling herself she would little appreciate the intrusion.

Just minutes later she had to look again. Same man, same chair, same position. But, something was different. She lowered her head over her book, keeping only her eyes on him. Noting his fair hair, and how his old, but neatly done, suit fit him.

Without seeming to move, he slowly produced a cigarette and lit it. Fascinated, she watched small clouds as he exhaled. Why did he hold her so? He was only of average size, so easily missed. Disconcerted, she gathered her things and left to spend the day wandering the unfamiliar streets.

It was hard to wake up. The night before she was restless, unable to sleep. In her dream there was something she should be doing, somewhere she should be. Always waking before the answer came. No sense trying to go back to bed, no matter the desire.

She dressed, made herself a light breakfast, and decided to go for a walk. She loved the small shops where everyone was so friendly. And the quiet shaded lanes.

Mid afternoon she stopped at a small café she preferred. The owner, a rather stout older woman, urged her to eat. Always saying, "You are too skinny."

There he was again. She was sure of it. It was getting late, and she best get back to her rooms. But now the chill followed her, making her walk faster. She was nearly home

when she passed him again. This time he acknowledged her, and tipped his hat.

Early next morning she woke feeling better. The day was grey and uninviting. She combed her short brown hair, and tried to dress to brighten her pale complexion—and maybe the dull day. After her breakfast she returned to her rooms. She hated being inside. It depressed her and left her with a sense of foreboding.

To fill the day she decided to read. Before she realized it, she had dozed off. The dream returned. This time the man across the way was there.

Why did something stir? What was just behind the fog? Her confusion was deepening.

2.

Upon waking she tried to interpret the dream. She had a feeling some parts were very real, but still floating in the mist.

It was still early enough for a walk to the little park nearby. She loved the peace and quiet of the small community green. She left the rooming house, turning left along her regular route, her mind wandering a little, concentrating.

Suddenly, sharply, she again felt an unreasonable chill. Why? Why should new construction on a vacant lot bother her? Some unfinished shop, or warehouse, behind a fence to protect the public. She needed to get to her little bench on the green, in the sun.

No sooner had she sat down and found her place in her book, than she heard a birdsong. Smiling and looking up, there he was across the park on another bench. He must be on vacation, too. Maybe she should welcome him. Then she decided against it. *Just to be still and wait.*

The following day started out clear and warm, the perfect day for a lunch in the woods. Her favorite café owner smiled in agreement, even sneaking in a few pastries with the bread, cheese, sausage, and wine.

She set off toward the edge of town, keeping to the narrow but well-traveled road, swinging her basket.

She had spread her blanket and was lying watching the sky, listening to the water and birds. Such lazy, lulling music. So relaxed, she hadn't noticed the dark clouds gathering and darkening.

The low rumbling thunder quickened her pulse. She sat up, staring around. Another rumble, a more frenzied search. A crack of lightening, with a louder rumble closer.

Panic! Grab the basket and blanket. Pelting rain, lightning, roaring thunder. *Run. Run. Hide. Hold tight. Get down. Area search.* Lightning—Thunder—*Run—Don't let go!*

Why?

They were getting closer. She could hear the shouts. *Must be quiet. Don't move.*

The roaring guns, the flashing explosions. *Keep them all quiet. Hush the baby. Please, God, don't let them find us.*

She sat huddled in the underbrush holding the blanket and basket as if life depended on it.

She felt hands on her shoulders. Some of the panic began to subside. She turned, somehow knowing it was the man across the way. She trusted him to gently take her and her basket home. With his strong arms around her, she began stumbling through the storm. His presence felt familiar. Memories set in.

Then she was safe, dry, and warm. She opened her eyes in her own bed. Turning her head slowly there sat Greta smiling through tears. And Karl, next to her, ashen, but looking relieved.

It was there—real—horribly real. The tears began, and so did the nightmare memories. The worrying turned to fear, then terror.

The scheme was far from simple or safe.

She and Karl were to meet their contact with another

group and next location. This was not the ordinary rescue; small children and a baby were among the refugees. They had started out pretending to be a young couple on a picnic. "Follow the lesser used path of five kilometers to a clearing, and wait until dusk. If the meeting didn't happen by then, return to town," as the happy couple.

3.

An older couple, tired and haggard; a young mother, thin and exhausted, with two small children, cold, hungry, and afraid; and a baby, not much older than four or five months.

The trade-off went as intended. Karl led the way stealthily through the woods heading west. She carried the baby in their basket. The mother carried the younger child, and the man carried the older. No names were used, for the safety of all concerned.

Just after it began to rain they found what was left of an old farm shed. Hoping it wouldn't rain long, they took shelter. But that had been a mistake. Tired, the children had fallen asleep, and the rain continued. They decided Karl, alone, would be less noticeable, and could maybe find some food.

He hadn't been gone very long when they heard first the dogs. *Run! Quiet—run.* Out of the shed into the cold brush.

The rumbling of the vehicles and the shouting! Orders given. Guns spitting death. Then the shells exploding!

The children were terrified into wide-eyed silence, but the baby cried. She could not quiet him. Over the noise of the battle, the crying of the baby was an unnatural sound. Try to sneak them away before the enemy gets too close. That was her job. That was her mission. To save as many of these poor souls as she and her team could. No names, just their leg of the journey.

Keep moving. Hold on. Don't let go.

Then they were in front of them. Nowhere to go.

"Halt!"

"Who are you?"

"Where do you think you are going?"

The woman panicked and tried to run. The guns began, the shouting of ugly slurs, and the flashing reports. The smell of powder and fear. The screams! The screams!

She ran, holding the basket for a dear life. Then all was hushed.

Why was the basket so sticky? Where was everyone?

Slowly, painfully, she sat up and looked back.

All dead. Five bodies, old and young, and an all-too-quiet basket.

That was where Karl must have found her.

Now she was here in her own bed, in her room with Aunt Greta and her friend Karl. It was all over. The enemy had lost. It would take a long time for the memories to heal. For the nightmares to fade.

But she was home in her village, safe, and loved.

THE ISLE FOR SICK MEN

My companion lay near death's door.
My mission must succeed.
I pushed on in a fevered frenzy.
The wave's rocking gave him small comfort
Pressing on through the darkness.

Then came such a moaning,
Such a weeping, and wailing.
My senses alerted, my heart pounding,
I bravely sailed on,
Pushing through the rough seas.
The destination was nearing.

Through the mist came the call.
"Halt! State your purpose."

"Permission to land, please.
My husband has a cold."

"Come ashore. He is welcome here.
See you in seven to ten days."

As I sailed home I gave a sigh
Of deep relief.
I said a silent prayer:
"Oh, thank the heavens for the
Isle for Sick Men."

THE LIFE OF BOWS

He fastened the bow tie perfectly, and with much aplomb. He was very proud of his appearance. Many saw him as a rather bland man, a bit on the plump side, not rally handsome. But he worked hard, and was well respected in his neighborhood. His colleagues believed him above average in his profession. This was an important night for him. His future depended upon it.

She smoothed the ribbon and tied back her dark auburn hair with the bow jauntily on one side. She judged herself in the mirror: small, too flat in all the wrong places. A smile that immediately made others at ease. Not terribly pretty, but attractive in the quiet way.

It's amazing how beautiful she was when he came to escort her for a walk.

She couldn't believe how lucky she was to be attended by such a handsome man.

A short distance into the park they sat and watched the stars. He produced a small velvet box tied with a yellow satin bow. Her eyes were radiant, and her smile told him his future was secure.

FISHIN'

"I could be fishin'," he thought.
He could feel the fish on the end of his line.
And taste the sweet reed stem he loved to
chew. The sun was warm, with a soft breeze
to keep the day comfortable. He could
almost hear the bees in their hive down by
the riverbank. It was a day for running
through tall grasses, and climbing trees.
Or a day to sit idle and daydream. So many
things to see and do on a fine day like today.

"Sold!"
The chains on his neck and wrist
said different.

Judy Womack

WHY I LIKE TO WRITE

My sixth grade teacher, Mrs. Stout, gave me the gift of wanting to write. She opened a whole new world for me by encouraging me to write stories. She said, "Write what is interesting to you. It doesn't matter if it's the start of a sentence. Just go for it."

I started writing poetry and short stories. One of the poems I wrote that won second place in the sixth grade:

Winter has gone
Spring is here
Birds are singing
Far and near.
Flowers are blooming
This time of year.
Isn't it nice
Spring is here?

THE MOUNTAIN

How long have I been sitting here,
looking out over this land?
How long has it been since I felt the footprints of man?
I watch the trees grow and I see them burn down
When the lightening strikes them to the ground.
Then I feel a spring-like kiss on my cheek
And I see that life has made it full circle
And it feels so sweet.

"Dudes, I Ate the Hunter"

First duck: "Wow, that tasted great. Why didn't we know hunters were so tasty?"

Second duck: "Well, dummy. All we ever eat are weeds and bugs. Now we can sneak around and sample during hunting season, and no on will know."

First duck: "Yeah, except for poor old Charlie, lying there. He died of a heart attack when he saw what we did. Hee, hee."

I Know the Sound of the Raven's Wing

Walking the forest I heard a strange sound.
Was it the wind blowing softly?
It sounded like something
flapping in the wind.

I kept looking up and saw nothing.
Was it the sound the trees made,
swaying to the earth's music?
It was a beautiful sound.

Finally, I saw it…
something very black
flew and landed in a tree.
A raven sat, looking down at me.

I didn't want to move or disturb it.
Yes, I know the sound of the raven's wings.

GRANDFATHER CLOCK
(POV Inanimate object)

I am two hundred years old, made in the 1800s, and am made of wood.

I have watched so many people pass me by, sitting alone in my corner. I've seen many children grow into adults, and have their families.

But now some wonders have come into my view.

Something called a computer. I hear someone say, "Well, I can see and talk to my cousins across the oceans."

Another says, "Oh, it can do my homework for me."

But the most interesting thing is the breakthrough of medicine, like doctors doing operations, conferring with another doctor in a foreign country.

I wonder if I could make it another hundred years, what would be happening in this world I have watched pass me by.

If only I could walk out of this house, and stand on the porch to really see the world.

HAVING AMNESIA

Flashes of light behind my eyes. I don't want to open them. There is a bit of a headache. Finally I open my eyes and look at my surroundings. Not familiar.

I get out of bed. I walk to the mirror. Stand there. "Who are you?" I ask the image in the mirror.

Panic. It hits me. *Why don't I know who you are?*

When I walk to the window, I see a town. But where? There are people riding on horses, and horses pulling buggies. *Where am I?*

A knock on the door. I say, "Come in."

A lady in a maid's uniform curtsies, and asks if I'd like breakfast.

Wait a minute. Am I hungry? I ask myself. *Maybe.*

I ask the maid, "Where am I?"

She gets a strange look on her face, and says, "My lady, you are at your town house."

"But where?" I ask.

She replies, "England."

"What?"

She says, "Yes, ma'am, it is. It's your wedding day."

"Wedding day!!" I exclaim. "To whom?"

"You just have wedding jitters, dear," the maid says as she smiles.

"Well, who am I marrying?"

She giggles. "Lord Prescott. He's the duke."

I jump into the bed. "No, it can't be! I don't think I'm supposed to be here." I pull the covers over my head.

The maid says, "I'm going for the doctor!"

"FRANKLY, I DON'T GIVE A DAMN"
—Scarlett O'Hara

I was a kid watching an old movie with my mom. She was a Clark Gable fan and she loved old Hollywood movie classics and westerns. We were watching *Gone With the Wind*. It was a rerun, of course. This one was in color, but my mom had first seen it in black and white.

This time with her was special because my mom worked a lot and it was rare for her to be able to sit down and watch a movie with me.

My mom influenced me about people. She was a kind person. She said, "You never know what people are dealing with." She fed strangers, for example she would bring coffee or water to someone working on our yard. She never judged appearances. She always told me not to judge people. I didn't.

LIFE IN THE TWILIGHT ZONE

She was driving on a lonely road. It was late. The road was winding, and she kept passing the same sign saying the town was only six miles ahead.

She went six miles. No town. At first she thought it was a joke. Another six miles ahead, still no town.

Finally, after twenty miles she came to a small café.

As she pulled in, she saw the name of the café was "The Town."

She got out and went inside. The response from a lady behind the counter was, "You found The Town."

IN THE NIGHT GARDEN

As I was taking my evening walk, I passed by an old house that looked empty. I was curious, so I opened the gate, walked carefully in, looking left and right. No one was about.

I went to the back of the old house. There were shrubs and bushes all around. In an opening I saw the most beautiful garden of flowers. They were everywhere, neatly surrounding a fountain showing Venus rising from the water.

I noticed a bench. I took out my phone to use it as a flashlight. Written on the bench were names and dates. One said, "To my darling, Esther. I will miss you so much. You are the love of my life."

It was dated 1860. And there, lying on the bench, was a fresh cut white rose.

THE DREAM

Black hair like raven wings that fly in the sky
Dark eyes like obsidian that would make a woman sigh.
Tall and beautiful he stands, proud like a mighty oak tree
Yet he walks through the forest silent and free.
This Indian who comes into my dreams
has courage of a lion through the night.
And when his eyes meet mine,
They strike my soul with a blinding light.
His kiss flows through me like a rushing river
His touch strong, yet gentle, makes me quiver.

Then I awake, but I remember.

SCOTLAND

Scotland—land of castles, kilts, and history.
Getting on a tour bus, waiting to board, anticipation.
My dream vacation.

Going off the beaten paths,
seeing parts of castles withered with age.
Wanting to stay longer to walk around and see,
but tour buses have their schedules to meet.

Tourists on the bus are from
many different places in the world.
Stopping at different places to eat, like old pubs.
Hearing the locals talking,
their brogue hard to understand.

But, I'm loving every minute.
Wish I had more time to stay and wander about.
But, always have to stay on their schedule.

One day I will come back and
enjoy all Scotland has to offer.

Eleni Zepeda

APRIL SNOW

The fallout of the fusion storm
Mixture in ash and snow
Springs last attempt to shower
Leaves plains of desolate sand
Ice hot to the touch
That melts the flesh from the bone
Wastes of emptiness
Vast and eerie
Residue in the aftermath
Of a last war
No remaining holdout to escape
Plasma left in the stratosphere
The weight of blackness drapes
Of a confused bleak atmosphere
Like a noose long hung
Without an o-zone layer to protect
The once live organism
They vanished in an agonized
Last breath of guilt and regret
Einstein said,
"I do not know with what weapons WWIII
Will be fought, but WWIV will be fought
With stick and stones!"

If enough are left to throw.

THE HILLS OF ETERNITY

The hills of eternity,
Amongst the palms
Overlooking the realm; the beyond.
Existentially mourning the human,
Malaise of yesterday,
Immortalizing the lives,
Into tomorrow.
The morrow where all,
Graves will be.
The morrow when,
We will all be free.
Released from this gravity,
Into the stardust of our eternity.

WHEN YOU LOOK INTO MY EYES

Shards of metal,
Bereft of meaning,
The points of an edge,
Has more purpose
For stabbing, for slicing…
What's left of a pure,
Psyche's flesh.
Rearranging puzzle pieces
Into a patchwork of code.
Reflections staring back,
Of a being
That was not there at birth,
But will remain
Until your last breath.

203

A MINUTE OF TERROR

When the day came my heart froze with burning anger. *How can people be so selfish?! How has it come to this? Or was it here all along?*

I stood in place like a statue when I saw the announcement. On my phone the announcement screamed, **"Emergency Alert!** Ballistic missile inbound to the western United States. Seek immediate shelter. This is not a drill."

I looked around me. Other people on campus were staring at their screens too—a look of disbelief in their eyes and on their faces. Some students reacted faster than others. I heard crying. One student yelled, "Fuck this!" and threw his notebook in the trash and then ran out of the building.

I felt clammy. *Move!* I screamed in my mind. *Damn it! Fucking move!* I realized I had blanked out. I was sitting in my van. I hadn't put the keys in the ignition yet. I shakily put them in and started the vehicle. I looked around. I thought crazily, *I better not die in a car accident on my way home.*

The streets were surprisingly jammed as I pulled off Crater Lake Highway trying to turn on to Summers Lane.

Is there enough time? How long does it take to get to a shelter? How long does it take to get to anywhere before the missile hits?

Then I had another crazy thought. *Is there much of a difference between a nuclear bomb and a ballistic missile?!*

For a moment it felt like the Doppler effect when I was driving. Everything was passing me by, but I felt slowed into a cone of perpetual panic. There was a deafness in my ears that went away as I started getting closer to home. I could hear again; a rush of motors flooding my senses.

I pulled into my driveway and ran inside my house, then grabbed my dog's leash and put it on him. Jupiter did not object. He sensed that something was up.

What am I going to do?! Am I going somewhere? Mom lives an hour away! Should I stay here and die in my home? I crumbled to the floor, cross-legged, not crying but in shock.

I checked my phone and realized it still worked—I hadn't checked the news since the alert came. Another automatic message had popped up. "False alarm. Repeat, no missile launched. False alarm!"

My eyes were stinging. I realized I had been crying. I went outside to look at the sky. No fighter jets where practicing, with the thunderous screech overhead like they usually do. Jupiter had followed me outside, his leash trailing behind him. Neighbors where coming out of their houses too, wary that the missile was a false alarm.

BLACK

A dark void into nothingness, an endless calm of the
unknown pitch.
That paralyzes the paths of humans at their height of
being.
A dimension on a parallel canvas of endless imagination
from the pit of the mind.
No limits to what can ignite the fears and wonder.
The creative landscape that scathes all boundaries into
oblivion.
Black: a paralyzing power that allows access into the very
phobias of man.
Unknowingness that enthusiastically hacks the control
center of the soul.
Tearing out the thirst of a howling ancestral animal that
splashes that canvas in a glory of defiance.

LUNACY

The full moon undid,
What civilization hid.
For so long the night tried to cover,
The animal's true nature.
Like the pull of the tide,
And the drop in the temperature,
Do we all wonder,
What is that scream in our minds?
With the swell of the orb,
Showing all our true textures.
The howl called us,
To our ancestors' ways.
A generational hunger,
That will refuse to go astray.

A Satire of War

Prt.1

When all is said and done,
The war is won,
The enemy's battle plan thrown,
The rejoicing shown.

After all is said and done,
There are no limits to what humans will do
To each other.
Thus, pardons will be after,
The prisoners are strung.

When all is said and done,
The soldiers, the heroes,
The winners, the reapers.

Because ***when all is said and done,***
Adaptations are for the ones left,
Because when the battle is over,
When the war is won,
The minds of hero's turn numb,
Their battle played out,
Their territories drawn,
Their families don't question....
Civilization moves on.

Prt.2

Before ***when all was said and done,***
The enemies are dehumanized,
The soldiers are moralized.

207

Fear is the fuel
That sparks the anger.
Propaganda demands:
To serve your country,
Proves you're braver.
While back home citizens stockpile
Supplies, food, and weapons.

When all was said and done,
"Everyone" would understand your reasons...
The government knows what is best,
Don't forget your Kevlar vest.
Just in case, build those bomb shelters.

Because **when all was said and done,**
Power with money will still be the system,
But espionage will be the reaction.

Because **when all was said and done,**
The People will be the victims,
They will want to know the government's reasons.
Why was the last defense digging for safety?
The Control insisted:
The nuclear weapons will bring us glory,
With "fire and fury" to the enemy!

Pt.3

When all is said and done,
No one knew...
Which side has won?
The military soon takes over....

When all is said and done,
Is it time for a coup?

Will the shelters be our graves?
Or will response be a catch-22?

When all was said and done,
Damned if we do...
Damned if we don't.
It's time to put away the battle drums.

MADNESS IN UNDERSTANDING...

People put their words into lyrics
So they can hide it between the instruments.
That way those who normally wouldn't want to listen
Will only realize until they dance to them.
Once they hear, it will be subliminally imbedded
In their subconscious.
No hiding behind the volume and the off-switch.
What people will dance to?
What song will try and express the musician's experience?
We try to comprehend the world we live in...
Music is a way to help the procedure along,
No matter how mad, no matter how insane.
We see the world with each step and breadth,
Write it all down so that those who are left
Can analyze the process. In doing so,
Understand the madness of life.

MORNING DECEMBER 1545

I suck in a long breath. It catches in a knot in my chest, then a lump in my throat. As I breathe out, it is noticeable by my exhale that the room is cold. Ice is creeping its way up the thick glass windows and I shiver despite the large fireplace that heats up the entire kitchen.

Each meal might be my last. I face uncertainty with trepidation and honor. I face these perils since I was convinced it would change the outcome of the country. If the Queen dies, then fate shifts once again on this grand chessboard of life. Is mine really worth a stable timeline? Must I sacrifice my existence for the Queen?

I am in the kitchen standing next to a thick wooden table with Her Majesty's next meal, ready to be carried out to her chambers. The other kitchen maids are expectant, waiting with fear in their eyes before I drink a sip of Merlot from a goblet made of silver. *Get it over with* I tell myself. I hold a wooden rosary in my left hand, my well-earned callused fingers counting the smoothness of each bead, even though I know it isn't worth it. I grip the handle of the goblet and press my lips to the rim. I take a cautious sip. The warm wine flows over my tongue and down my throat. I realize my hand is trembling, while I take my last sip. I open my eyes realizing I also had closed them while swallowing the wine.

I look around; I am still here, I am standing. No poison to worry about.

But the suspense is not over. Next, the golden-brown hue of the croissant and off white yellow of butter come into my vision. I put the goblet down on the tray and the rosary I give to one of the kitchen maids, who takes it with a look of surprise. I am more confident now, if the wine isn't poisoned the meal might not be. I take a piece of the warm flakey croissant and spread the soft butter on it. I place the tantalizing bite in my mouth and let the warm flakes last on my tongue as the butter melts.

I swallow. I am still here.

Next, the fruit. Oranges for this meal, with slices of apples. I swallow the citrus-flavored fruit, rare and expensive this time of year. I sway a bit. I think it is probably strychnine poisoning. The taste could be masked by the bitter citrus.

One of the maids gasps, while another rushes forward to help me balance.

"I am fine! I say. I am just overcome with relief."

She backs away.

I take a slice of apple. I bite into it. *Crunch*. It is sweet with a hint of pear, the color yellow. I am still here... standing. My larynx isn't closing, my nose and eyes are not bleeding. I have no foam frothing or blood gushing from my mouth and no signs of sudden jerks or convulsions. I was warned, from the royal physician, these are the symptoms of many poisons.

The breakfast tray is ready to be carried to Her Majesty's chamber. That is not my task though. The queen doesn't want to meet her "sacrifice" of the day. She doesn't have to worry about the end of her life...for now. If I back out of this now, I will be replaced and another will be sacrificed. Each new meal holds the fate of the country at risk. I am just a lowly pawn trying to block the enemies from my Queen.

KLAMATH BASIN WRITERS

Perri Zepeda

A GODDESS HEART

If I were a goddess, my steps would be soft and peaceful on the Earth.

The animals of the forests, meadows, and waters would know me as benevolent. Each creature would share their wisdom with me so that I might pass on their stories and lessons.

If I were a goddess, people would feel safe and loved in my presence. People of every walk of life would find they could open their heart and talk to me, and I would listen with respect. I would know their truths from falsehoods, as owls can see in the dark.

If I were a goddess, I would speak with humility as an equal to all other souls, affirming each of our lives have manifested from the same source.

INTO THE LIGHT
(Inspired by life and death)

"You still here?" Mom squeezes my hand.

Without opening my eyes, I see my mother's image, her aura.

She breathes deeply, sighing, and humming a song, her own.

I whisper, "Yes, Mama. I am grateful for you in my life. For your everlasting love. For always being there for me."

"I love you, Perri. When you leave this plane, I will know you are present always in my heart, in my thoughts." She holds my hand, soft and warm. "The fragrant breeze of flowers will make me think of you."

"I believe so, Mama. We will be together again on the other side." My heart beats a slow rhythm. I feel safe.

The room is peaceful in afternoon sunlight.

"I will still talk with you, Perri. We can talk anytime. I will still need you. Your love, your strength, your wisdom." My mother leans in, resting a warm hand on my shoulder.

"Oh, Mama, thank you for guiding me, and caring for me, for being the best example of a mother. You are the most trusting love a person could want or need."

Mom returns to her song, holding my hand in her hands.

Tingling, I become LIGHT. I become LOVE . . .

Into the LIGHT, I am FREE.

ANYTIME, GRANDMA, I AM HERE

"Trista, something tells me you're here with me. Your spirit. Your voice. I hear your voice, and I can talk to you."

"Yes, Grandma, I'm here. I have missed you these last few years."

"Hey, I was just thinking the same thing. You don't know how I have grieved not having you and your brother in my life, in our lives. You have been 13, 14, and now, 15 years old. You are mature. You had to know the adults in your life sure have had their problems and misunderstandings that prevented us from seeing each other or talking on the phone. You do know you are not responsible for these problems."

"Yes, I know. I have watched and listened to each and every one. All of you. I have known the truth. I have known you still loved me and my brother. I know how it was not possible for you to be in our lives. I know what caused this."

"A few years ago, when I wanted to put on a Girl's Camp at the ranch, and you weren't allowed to come, I grieved something awful knowing I was cut off from you. I told myself, *I guess I have to wait until Trista is 18 and she can make her own decisions. She can call me and see me then.* I even wrote you a letter I never sent. I titled it, 'On my deathbed.' In case I never saw you again, I would have that letter left behind for you expressing my love for you and your brother."

"Grandma, we have each other now. Anytime. I know it isn't the same, but you can talk to me anytime. You can even read me stories and poetry you write, out loud, like we used to do. And I will share mine. I will have plenty to say about how life was and how it is on this side. I love you, Grandma."

"Thank you, Trista! I love you forever!"

*RIP Trista Renee Hoffman 8-3-2001 – 10-21-2016

TWILIGHT ZONE
"THE POWER OF HEIGHTS"
Episode 58

In a distant realm, a lone girl wanders along a lush ravine. Her step is light and quick, her breathing measured, as her eyes scan the ground of moss-covered stones and fallen dead firs.

Ahead, a roaring waterfall nurtures the rich, green earth. She rinses her hands, face, and feet. Eager to drink, the cold water shocks, shivering her empty belly. As the water stills, her reflection becomes clear. She stares back at herself, lost in a dream, releasing a deep breath.

There she rests on a flat, smooth boulder, swishing her feet in a shallow pool. The water gurgles, spraying an iridescent peppermint mist over her. The sun beats down, burning her skin, steaming her thin, wet dress.

Tiny stars fill the water around her, casting every color of the rainbow. Multiplying, they rise from the pool and join together in a ball of fire in front of her. Flames spark and ignite into the form of a flying emerald carpet.

Ahhh... Never before has she seen such an occurrence. She stands and steps back. Mesmerized, she gazes into the hovering blanket, settling down at her feet.

A kind voice whispers, "Sit upon this place before you. You will be transported to the highest heights above the terrestrial zone. You will understand your world from above."

Safe? I don't know.

She hesitates, then steps forward. In a split second, she is gone with the ephemeral carpet. On the boulder baking in the sun, her wet footprints disappear.

217

THE PRIDE YOU TRAMPLED

Heavy footsteps rattled the old back porch and stopped short of the kitchen screen door.

Henrietta paced inside sucking her eleventh Pall Mall cigarette out of her second pack since supper. She glanced at the kitchen door to the backyard, waiting. Burning mad, she stubbed her half-smoked cigarette out in the ceramic ashtray overflowing with butts.

How dare he come home at this hour? The round, red-hen, clock clucked twelve times for midnight. *Damn, Sal!*

The screen door grinded open. The kitchen door knob twisted.

Henrietta poured another shot of whiskey down her throat.

Like a scared cat, the door flew open, screeching, and slammed against sacks of potatoes and grain.

"Kick the devil! Why did I ever marry you?!" She squeezed the lifeblood out of her fists.

"Darlin', you just like your mother. A bitter bitch. You'll trample my pride no more!" He stumbled past her.

That's when she knew the relationship was over. Yes. That was the last time she would tolerate the women.

* * * * *

Her rage had propelled her to scrub, sweep, mop, cook . . . and alas, calm down with mending and singing lullabies to her children. Alone most days, she tried to console herself.

I deserve better. I am so embarrassed to admit this. I'd rather those women would keep him occupied and draw

his attention away from me and the children. Oh, the poor children worship their papa and long for his company. If only he treated them like they mattered and spent time playing with them! He makes an appearance, flies in, drops off chocolates and the latest toy fad. Kisses their heads. Spews broken promises and grumbles on and on . . .

When he made an appearance, the children would squeal, "Papa! Papa!" and leap to embrace him. "You haven't even seen my model rocket! Or played with the kitty! Please stay and play!"

As quick as he entered the home and whirled around the children, he disappeared out the side door. *Slam!*

The children would freeze, staring at the ghost at the door. Hanging their heads, they wept. Toys flew.

* * * * *

I never want to see him again. This time, I am leaving with the children. We are not his property. He shall feel relieved. He can have all the women he wants. That beast! And my children and I will begin our new life adventure far out of his reach.

She pauses in front of the fireplace mantel. *Oh, no! Our family portrait. There. So lovely. We appear happy . . .*

No! I will cut him out and replace him with a tall, kind, and gentle animal. Or, perhaps a plant. A big beautiful flower. A purple petunia. Trampled pride . . . Humpf!

ONE SEED'S BEGINNINGS

My life started when I was an itty-bitty seed. My earliest memories . . .

My eyes, closed—heavy, as at the end of a deep sleep, before fully conscious and in a calm trance, I floated inside of a veiled, protective capsule, safe and light.

I didn't know what would happen next or what I would do; the plan was in place before my time. I sensed both ease and rumblings of change, my being vibrated in a gentle dance of transformation.

Around me and at my sides, an invisible energy tugged at my outer shell. Tawny gold melted away from me.

A deep urge shifted me to stretch toward the sky, levitated, drawn and empowered by an enormous fireball in the Great Beyond. I opened my eyes, portals to an extraordinary scene both separate and a part of me. Dense clouds glided across a vast, heavenly expanse, coating me in cool moisture. Like a shriveled, spongy mushroom, I absorbed the nectar drink. Wee! —A wild gust of wind lifted me, escorting me to the elevations of wise eagles I would come to know.

And there below, a world of wonder . . . I could have never imagined: A spread of brilliant flowers radiated, glowing of joy and welcome, a sea of greens, rippling, swaying.

Down, down I swirled, feeling light, anticipating the beautiful world where I would live, where I would grow.

Landing in softness, I sensed cool earth humming with life. Insects of unique designs carried on their life's mission with a knowing purpose. I rolled over inclined to rest, patient for an enormous and ambitious next adventure.

Determined ants marched around me carrying burdens of wood splinters and luminescent water bubbles. Industrious creatures, they built a shelter over me. All went dark.

I breathed deep into my core. Eyes closed, waiting for whatever would come. My inner voice, my soul, was ready.

A whisper reassured me, *Peace . . . peace . . .*

I let go of expectation, trusting.

IMAGINE
(Inspired by John Lennon's song)

Imagine higher consciousness for everyone.
Imagine we are all our boundless,
collective creativity for good.
Imagine what we can do alone and together
multiplying our positive effect on each other
and our precious Earth.
We love, not hate.
We are united, not divided.
We help, not hurt.
Imagine we give of ourselves in small ways that make a day,
fill a heart, change a person's outlook
so she or he may delight in new thought.
Imagine healing for everyone, with awareness and curiosity
accessing our gifts to channel vibrant wellness.
Imagine the courage to be loyal,
to be who we can be at our best.

PRIMAL LANDSCAPES
STRIPPED AND RAW

To my brother

In the woods I wander, breathing, feeling light.
My eyes set on the glow and shades of greens, the shapes
and patterns.
I feel the pulse of life singing here.

I reflect on why I am still alive today,
have the family I was born into,
and the children I have.

I have you, my brother.
You do your life as you wish in the moment, day after day.
You are creative and curious, appearing too alone in your
own world.

I return to our mother's where you are.
Her love and beauty fill her home and surroundings—
a striking contrast to the hurt and pain I feel.
A malevolent rift tore you and me apart once again.
I care not to engage and be shut down.

You and I do not talk, but we are near.
You carry on like I am a ghost.
. . . as if never hurting another,
never emitting crushing, harsh words.
    But, you know.
    I know.
    The truth.

I am not bitter, a putrid, mad lemon.
I need no approval.
I am not waiting for you to be ready for the
door I have left open.
I have no fight in me for wasted loving gestures.
Lose-lose serves no good purpose.
I only bargain for a win-win, equal footing,
and nothing less—
no hierarchy of superior-inferior posturing.
   "It is nice to feel important,
   but it is more important to be nice."

Will you ever fall on your knees, humble?
Cry a primal cry?
Will you ever know *that* metamorphosis?
   Releasing ego's fear and pomp.
   Knowing your pain is not more important
   than another's pain.
   Learning compassion and forgiveness for yourself first.
   Healing shame.
Your loneliness is in your head—I am here,
still alive on this Earth.
What could be of us as brother and sister
is a beautiful bond.
I once knew what that felt like.
Ask the Great Universe:
   What must I do?
   I am ready, let me see, let me know.
   We are Brother and Sister, Sister and Brother . . .

   . . . for I will be gone,
      in a single breath . . .

Rise Above It, Guidance From Within
(Inspired by the writings of the late Ernie Pecci. RIP)

My Question:
What actions do I need to take to shift the nature of conflicts as they arise in any or all of my relationships?

Meditation:
I sit in silence for several moments, clear my mind.

The Answer:
Remember this . . . As a human being, you have extraordinary gift-potential beyond your conscious sight and awareness. Within your reach and ability, there are affirmations you must use until they are integral to your immediate conscience. These affirmations will become instinctual and at your command.

In every moment, you have an opportunity to be conscious of your breath as you can be conscious of your thoughts and actions. Your beliefs either lead you to healthy thoughts and actions, or not.

At any given moment of a conflict, you must keep your center of calm being, a sacred place of peace and healing. You channel wisdom from the Great Universal Loving Mind directly to the wisdom of your heart-and-soul-mind. Every conflict is an opportunity to bring light and love and unity to the situation, engendering a creative force for healing, growth, and positive change.

All those souls around you need and want personal growth and evolution, and too often human emotions like anger and fear shield the possibility and hope of mutually beneficial solutions.

Listen to their hearts. Listen to their needs and wants. You will know what is fair-handed.

Grow yourself. Keep growing. You are on a path of revolutionary growth and healing.

Others who are open and ready, who love you, who learn to love themselves, will realize the only way forward is with this intention: Love, healing, and equality are for everyone. Humans are all in this together. The lines must be drawn for healing over harm, for protecting your whole being, for the greater good. The direction must be clear for growth, for equity in relationships.

Take care of yourself first, and you will have more clarity and strength to know how to think through and say and do what brings truth to light. You will understand and respect how choices can impact yourself and others with important, timely lessons and gifts.

TIME TRAVEL

I awake on the ground, a place of scattered rocks and water-carved furrows in the earth.

I leap to my feet and circle in all directions. *Where am I?* All mountain above, a wide green valley below.

I have never been here or seen the beauty like this before my eyes.

Enormous bright clouds hover at the peaks above. Steam rises around me.

I secure my footing, crunching in sinking gravel.

The valley breeze collides with a gust of wind from above me.

A woven backpack weighs me down. I feel curious what is inside. I drop my sack and open it. A colorful rolled tight blanket. A leather bag for a drink? Bananas and avocados.

Here, before me, is a spectacular place on Earth. I see no sign of other people, buildings, or roads. No evidence of the modern world.

I stand tall and breathe deep. I stretch. I breathe and stretch, free.

Not far away, faint percussion beats and singing echo. Joyful. Children's giggles and squeals rise and fade. I want to know who plays and sings, to see what is happening.

I move forward to follow the voices, the drumming. A narrow path winds around the rocky crevices thrusting towards the sky. With caution, I step in the sinking sand, pebbles cascade into the depths of a dark canyon of dense forest below.

I climb a rocky staircase. Steam blinds me and wisps away in rhythmic gales.

I can clearly see now, I have arrived to an open space of flat rock against the stone mountain.

There before me are a dozen children playing in a natural pool of hot spring water, singing with large smiles and bright eyes.

Elders stand and sit against the backdrop of the strong mountain wall, rapping on drums, shaking rattles and beads.

On the wall: pictographs . . .large lizards, people on boats, water, drumming, birds, the sun, mountains.

I don't understand their words. I sit down.

One boy points at me.

The people turn to look at me.

I smile.

They smile back and continue to play and sing.

I want to know these people. I want to learn from them. I want to befriend.

KLAMATH BASIN WRITERS

ABOUT THE AUTHORS

Toni Bailie

Toni Bailie hosts the Easy Writers group at her home in Paisley, Oregon. She was a magazine editor for Northwest Public Power Association. Her work was published in *Seasons, A Lake County Anthology* and *A Sense of Place,* an Eastern Oregon Anthology. She writes feature stories for *Ruralite Magazine* and a monthly column for *The Community Breeze.*

Erin Barker

Erin Barker didn't realize she was a writer when she and her twin sister wrote their first song at eight years old. Even after completing her first book at ten, she didn't understand the impact writing would eventually have on her life. Today, Erin uses writing to understand and artfully express the challenges that have shaped her.

Homesteading on Bly Mountain for over a decade, raising a son with autism, living with lifelong chronic pain, and more, have allowed her to see the world through lenses of compassion and understanding. She converts these experiences into gentle messages of faith, truth, goodness, and hope.

It is her hope her words included in this volume somehow tell you exactly what you need to hear.

Brian Ellis

Brian grew up in the Northern Baja town of San Diego, writing from the age of six. He eventually earned degrees in both Writing and Geography. As Geography is known to lead to a career path as either a teacher or someone who overthrows small, foreign governments, he chose to pursue writing. He ditched his career as a Realtor/Karaoke Junkie and leapt into a world he had always loved, that of film and television. Brian has been involved in successful, award-winning, low-budget independent features, and has multiple television shows in development, as both a writer and a producer, and just completed shooting his first film as a producer: Stitched to Perfection.

Mark H. Gaffney

Mark H. Gaffney is the author of five books. His articles, op-eds, poetry, and essays have appeared in many journals and magazines, in several newspapers, and are widely posted on the Internet.

Kei Oni Garcia

Kei Oni Garcia is a young author and poet, born and raised in Klamath Falls. She has been writing since elementary school. She has written dozens of poems and is working on her first full length novel.

Liz Garcia

Liz sold her first paintings and produced work on commission while still in high school. After graduating with Honors and the Art Award, she continued art studies in college, later attending the Academy of Art in San Francisco. Liz paints in acrylic, enjoying the variety of effects this medium is capable of. She loves exploring creativity through writing, painting, and music.

"Everywhere I look, I am entranced by the magnificence of the world and its creatures. Capturing that beauty in words or on canvas has been my life's inspiration."

Andie Icenbice

Andie Icenbice is a young author from Klamath Falls. They focus mostly on poetry and have a book published under the pen name Limerancy. They also write novels under the name A.J. Alastairs.

Jo Johnston

Jo Johnston's writing career began with a book of fiction, *Beyond Solitude: A Cache of Alaska Tales*. Several of her essays and works of poetry appear in various anthologies and collections. In addition to her passion for writing, Jo is a freelance editor, proofreader, book designer, writing instructor, and mentor. She works with established authors, and has helped many first-time writers see their dreams fulfilled. She lives in Klamath Falls, Oregon with her author husband, Ken Johnston.

Ken Johnston

Kenneth Johnston is a retired educator and author. In 2012, he published a book titled *Legendary Truths: Peter Lassen and His Gold Rush Trail in Fact and Fable*. In 2018 he published *The Nobles Emigrant Trail*. He is currently working on his next book, *Two Boomers on A Beemer* about his adventures and conjectures of riding his BMW motorcycle in the U.S., Canada, and China.

Ken has been actively involved with Oregon and California Historic Trails since 1974, when he was hired by Lassen National Park to develop a living history program to interpret the development of the Lassen and Nobles Trails, which are closely associated with the National Park. He continues to enjoy exploring emigrant trails, and traveling the world. He and his wife, Jo live in Klamath Falls, Oregon.

Leigh Lane

Leigh M. Lane has been writing dark sci-fi and horror for nearly thirty years. Although most of her works carry elements of dystopian and psychological horror, she's not averse to delving into the gritty and the extreme. Her most prominent influences are Serling, Matheson, Vonnegut, Orwell, Wells, Bradbury, Poe, King, Rice, and Dahl. For more information about Leigh and her works, visit her website at http://www.cerebralwriter.com.

Laura Larsen

Laura Larsen is a Southern California transplant to the Basin and is pleased to watch the growth and development of this town. She is the author of Facing the Final Mystery: A Guide to Discussing End-of-Life Issues, and is currently writing a memoir. She enjoys gardening and reading, as well as editing and transcribing via TrifectaTEC.com

Marie Lee

Marie Simms Lee was raised on the Simms Ranch in the Valley Falls area of Lake County, Oregon. She has self-published non-fiction books about her life on the ranch, *The Way We Were in Valley Falls*, *At the Ranch Beneath the Rim*, a children's book, *Cowgirl Lessons*, and a historical novel about her grandmother's life, *The View From God's Country*. She occasionally writes poetry as a delightful reprieve. She is retired from Fremont-Winema National Forest and makes her home in Lakeview—not too far from the old ranch.

Doug Matheson

Doug Matheson grew up a missionary kid in India, and was educated in Christian schools until graduate school. He taught in Lebanon in 1980-81, and did public

health work in Rwanda from 1991 to April of 1994 and the beginnings of the genocide. He taught in Oman in 2017-18, and spent many years working and discussing things right here in America.

He has taught science and then socials in southern Oregon, creating an elective called Global Issues. He founded Klamath Basin Youth Without Borders, published *Actually THINKING vs. just BELIEVING*, and founded Klamath Basin FreeThinkers.

He tries to integrate and balance being an informed, concerned, and constructively involved citizen. He identifies his most vital self-evident truth as this: We owe a decent, stable, and enjoyable planet to future generations.

Crystal Moreno

Raised in a nomadic family who loved the adventure of travel. Crystal has made Klamath Falls home base for thirty years. She fell in love with and married a local boy and did all the wonderfully prosaic things that comprise a well lived life: raising a family, buying property, and having a fulfilling career. After an early retirement, she lost her sanity and decided to go back to college and finish her degree.

Crystal has a variety of interests, including but not limited to: volunteer work, animals, the great outdoors, and the comfortable indoors. She enjoys people who are deeply compassionate and possess the ability to curse creatively. Crystal is, herself, passionate about the subject of writing. She enjoys challenging subjects, socio-political allegory, prose, poetry, and fiction.

Jim Olson

Jim Olson grew up in northern Illinois and moved to central California during high school. After graduation he joined the US Navy and served two tours in Viet Nam. Later he became a truss designer and was moved all over the country. Jim wrote his first book in 2000 and was hooked. He moved to Klamath Falls in 2009 right after retirement.

Alex Spenser

Alex Spenser is a writer, motivational speaker, and coach of writing, life, relationship, and performance. She believes in the possibility of peace, and that there is poetry in all things and in all times. Please visit Alex at: www.WordsWithWings.com

Cathy Williams

Cathy Williams was born in South Dakota and lived there until she was seven. Her family moved to Oregon where her dad worked on a ranch for a few years. They ended up in Portland, where Cathy lived until 1972 when she and her husband moved to Hawaii for five years.

Cathy started writing stories at the age of about five or six. She says, "I have always been told I have a very active imagination, and I think that helps with my writing. I write mostly verse, and a very few short stories. Much of what I write comes on the spur of the moment, and kind of takes over until I put it down on paper."

She's been a member of the Klamath Basin Writers for five years. She says, "The group is amazing when it comes to helping each other with their chosen form of talent."

Judy Womack

Judy Womack is the youngest of six girls and the first to go to college. She is a movie buff, and loves to read. She says, "It takes me into worlds I've never been in."

Judy has been married forty-seven years, and has two adult living children; she lost a daughter to a tragedy a few years ago.

"I've been through a lot, traveled through much of the U.S, but one day I dream of traveling out of the county."

She likes writing stories and poems, and hopes others enjoy them.

Eleni Zepeda

Eleni graduated from Oregon Institute of Technology in Klamath Falls, with a bachelor's degree in psychology and a minor in communication. She continued to write during college as a hobby. By volunteering she has become more involved in the community. She plans to publish a book of poetry and continue her education in the field of public health.

Perri Zepeda

Perri Zepeda is the author of the life skills workbook, *Jumpstart Your Life! Making Friends and Peace With Your Life Business*, designed for youth and adults and for diverse settings. She teaches a class using the workbook.

Soon to be published, is her memoir/fiction book addressing racism, the creation of worldviews, and the history of civil rights in the U.S., targeting both general audiences and educational settings.

Her first love for writing began at age thirteen when she wrote *A Pig's Tale* and later another children's book, *Vilcabamba*. She enjoys being a beta reader via TrifectaTEC.com. Perri is a member of the Klamath Basin Writers' Group and hosts Writers and Art Retreats on the ranch where she lives in southern Oregon.

Some of the athors: Standing Kei Oni Garcia, Jo Johnston, Jim Olson, Eleni Zepeda, Judy Womack. Seated Andie Icenbice, Brian Keith Ellis, Lainee Meis, Mark Gaffney, Perri Zepeda, Alex Spenser. Right front Laura Larsen.

Made in the USA
San Bernardino, CA
13 December 2018